The Fab Five
Jordyn Wieber, Gabby Douglas
and the U.S. Women's Gymnastics Team

GymnStars Volume 3

CREATIVE MEDIA, INC.
PO Box 6270
Whittier, California 90609-6270
United States of America

www.CREATIVEMEDIA.NET

Cover and Book design by Joseph Dzidrums

First Edition: July 2012

Library of Congress Control Number: 2012912532

ISBN 978-1-938438-09-7   10 9 8 7 6 5 4 3 2 1

The Fab Five
Jordyn Wieber, Gabby Douglas
and the U.S. Women's Gymnastics Team

GymnStars Volume 3

Biography by
Christine Dzidrums

Love to
Joshua, Timothy and Ashley

Table of Contents

"There's so much art in gymnastics. Each event is different in its own way. Vault is a really powerful event. Beam is a little more artistic. Floor where you can just go out there and dance along with the tumbling. I love the different elements of the sport."

"Jo"

On July 12th, 1995, one year before the Atlanta Olympics, Rita and David Wieber welcomed a bouncing baby girl into the world. The joyous couple named their daughter Jordyn, which means 'descend' or 'flow down'.

Tiny Jordyn was the third Wieber child. Older sister Lindsay and elder brother Ryan doted over their younger sister. Four years later, Jordyn became a big sibling herself with the birth of her sister Kyra.

The Wiebers quietly settled in DeWitt, Michigan. The small Midwestern town, nestled along the 71-mile Looking Glass River, offered quiet living, quality schools and a family-friendly community.

"I really like living in a small town," Jordyn later recalled. "Everybody knows everybody. It's just really nice."

With their new baby in tow, Dave forged a career in the health care industry, while Rita began working as a freelance writer and ER nurse. One eventful afternoon, Dave was dressing 11-month-old Jordyn on her changing table. Suddenly she stood up on one leg like a flamingo so he could slip her pant leg on.

"We'd already had two kids, so I knew that was unusual," Dave told *ESPN*. "She couldn't even walk, but she had this uncanny sense of balance."

A robust toddler, Jordyn rarely tired when playing. In fact, family members were often left exhausted just trying to keep up with her! Hoping to channel her daughter's boundless energy, Rita enrolled Jordyn and herself in a Mommy and Me gymnastics class. Right away, the young girl showed natural flexibility and remarkable balance.

Before long, Jordyn graduated into her own gymnastics class. The tiny tumbler enjoyed wearing a shiny leotard, gathering her dark brown hair into a high ponytail and learning exciting skills on all four gymnastic apparatuses: vault, balance beam, uneven bars and floor exercise.

Jordyn also exhibited a strong work ethic that belied her tender age. When the determined gymnast struggled with a skill, she practiced it repeatedly until finally mastering it.

Jordyn's Game Face
(Samantha Crawford)

By the time Jordyn reached age seven, she excelled in competitive gymnastics. Jo, as family and friends called her, loved showing off for a captive audience – the bigger the crowd, the better.

"Sometimes before competitions I would have dreams I was competing," Jordyn recalled. "My mom would say in the hotel room I'd be moving all around my bed in my sleep just because I'd be doing gymnastics in my mind."

"I remember her coach said she'd never seen a girl that age so intense," Rita added.

At age eight, Jordyn entered the Early State Championships and won gold medals in every apparatus! Her large collection of ribbons, medals and trophies overcrowded her display case at home!

Not surprisingly, Jordyn loved going to the gym every day. She trained a few miles from home at Geddert's Twistars in Lansing, Michigan. Husband and wife, John and Kathryn Geddert, served as her coaches. Their student's unparalleled concentration floored them.

"When we went 'wow' was when she started competing," John recalled. "When she was in the spotlight she brought out her best performances. A lot of people fold under pressure; she craves that sort of situation."

"I think her gift is her focus," Rita agreed when talking to *ESPN*. "From that very young age, she could get into a zone and nothing would distract her."

In summer of 2004, the nine-year-old soaked up television coverage of the Athens Olympics. The gymnastics competition particularly mesmerized her.

"I remember watching Carly Patterson win the all-around," she revealed. "I just thought it was the coolest thing ever, and I knew I wanted to be like her someday."

Just two years later, Jordyn became an elite gymnast herself. The proud athlete's heart swelled at the prospect of representing her country in international competition.

In summer of 2006, Jordyn competed against America's best junior gymnasts at the Visa Championships. In a strong field of 32 competitors, Jordyn finished an impressive 9th in the all-around competition.

One year later, Jordyn returned to nationals with high hopes of medaling. After all, she had upgraded several skills and carried more experience. In the end, the rising gymnast left the competition with four medals, including bronze in the all-around.

Later that season, USA Gymnastics named Jordyn to the Junior Pan America team. The ecstatic tween flew to Guatemala for her first international competition. In the end, she helped the United States win team gold and also scored four individual medals.

Jordyn enjoyed socializing with her teammates. When the girls weren't competing or sightseeing, they usually gathered together in a room and bonded.

"We do all the typical girl stuff," Jordyn revealed. "We do our nails. We like to listen to music."

As much as Jordyn enjoyed traveling, she always felt happy to return home. Nothing beat the comfort of sleeping in her own bed, which she sometimes shared with her dog Lucy.

When Jordyn wasn't on the road, she followed a strict schedule. She practiced every weekday morning, attended school for a few hours in the afternoon and returned to the gym for an evening workout.

"I like being a normal student," Jordyn revealed to *ESPN*. "I think it's cool to get to be an elite gymnast and go to school. It's good for the next generation to see. It keeps you balanced."

With such a rigid routine, an athlete needs immeasurable support. The Wiebers definitely lived up to the demands, and the family's star gymnast never took their help for granted.

"My mom and my family have been so great through my whole gymnastics career," Jordyn gushed. "From the very beginning, they've driven me to practice every single day, every day of the week. They've made so many sacrifices just so I can follow my dreams and reach my goals."

Meanwhile, the Wiebers were so proud of Jordyn. They enjoyed helping her pursue her career.

"99% of it has been a labor of love," Rita remarked. "It's been a great ride."

Although Mom supported her daughter wholeheartedly, she stayed out of her daughter's gymnastics business. She entrusted John and Kathryn to supervise her daughter's training.

"I leave the pushing to the coaches," she said. "I make sure she's fed and sleeping and give her all the support she needs. The coaches can do the pushing."

"When I drove the carpool, I dropped Jordyn off and picked her up when practice was over," Dave agreed when he spoke to *ESPN*. "Some parents sit for hours watching practice, and it's not healthy. I would never stay and watch my son play football. Once I drop him off, it's up to the coaches to coach him."

Although Jordyn's parents were very supportive of her career, they also refused to grant her any special treatment. They expected their daughter to help out at home and perform her own housekeeping duties.

"I don't do her laundry for her," Rita announced. "Now I kind of feel guilty because all of these other Olympic mothers say they do their child's laundry, but I don't! She has to do it."

When twelve-year-old Jordyn arrived in historic Boston, Massachusetts, for the 2008 Visa Championships, the determined competitor set her sights on winning the all-around gold medal. When the competition ended, she had accomplished her lofty goal! In addition, she also took first place on the floor and vault.

"She's a go-getter, a daredevil, not afraid of anything," John told *International Gymnast Magazine* after his student won. "But mentally, she's off the charts. When she gets in competition she doesn't see anything but the equipment. She's a competitor."

After the junior competition ended, Jordyn attended the senior ladies event. As the wide-eyed gymnast sat in the stands watching Shawn Johnson, Nastia Liukin and Alicia Sacramone perform their routines, she noticed that the superstars displayed unparalleled aggressiveness and confidence in their routines. She immediately vowed to emulate those qualities when she competed, too.

That summer Jordyn eagerly watched the 2008 Beijing Olympics on TV. The United States girls' gymnastics squad entered the games as favorites to win the team competition. However, they made several mistakes in the final and the team settled for silver. After the competition, Jordyn turned to her mom and declared with steely determination, "That's OK. We'll get 'em in 2012."

Unfortunately, a series of injuries plagued Jordyn the next two seasons. First a hamstring injury forced her out of the 2009 Visa Championships. Then on day one of 2010 nationals, she injured her ankle and reluctantly withdrew from the competition. The frustrated gymnast wondered if she would ever be healthy to compete again.

"It was pretty frustrating," she told the *Star Tribune*. "I had to be really patient with myself, especially with such a serious injury."

"It was hard for me, especially because I just love being in the gym working on my skills," she continued. "You have to just remember what your goals are and keep moving forward, remembering why you're doing this and how much I love gymnastics. That motivated me to keep going."

Despite the unwelcome setbacks, Jordyn maintained a positive outlook. It helped that her favorite song was "Life's What You Make It" by Miley Cyrus. The popular anthem urges people to keep a positive attitude no matter how frustrating life can be. The teenager often listened to the song when she needed a reminder to keep her spirits up.

During her down time, Jordyn rested at home. She entertained herself by watching recordings that brought her comfort. Her favorite movie? *Little Miss Sunshine*. Meanwhile, the drama series *Grey's Anatomy* ranked as the television show she liked the most. She also counted the reality TV series *Dance Moms* as a guilty pleasure.

Thankfully, the 2011 season brought a healthy Jordyn. The year also marked a major change for the teenager. She would now compete as a senior gymnast.

In early March, Jordyn flew to Jacksonville, Florida, to compete at the AT&T American Cup. The strong competitor wowed the crowd by narrowly defeating world champion Aliya Mustafina from Russia to take the all-around title.

Later that season, wearing a fittingly gold leotard, Jordyn arrived at the Xcel Energy Center in St. Paul, Minnesota, for her first senior nationals. Due to her strong performances all season, she entered the competition as the heavy favorite. The heavy expectations did not faze her, nor did she let them overwhelm her.

"It would be such an honor to be the national champion," she told the *Star Tribune*. "But right now, I'm just focusing on doing one thing at a time."

At the weekend's end, Jordyn had earned gold medals in the all-around, uneven bars and floor exercise. The girl who began gymnastics as a way to work off her extra energy now carried the title of America's top ranked gymnast!

"I had a lot of fun and I'm glad it turned out good," Jordyn told a reporter after the competition. "It was really exciting."

Jordyn's steady composure under pressure at the Visa Championships impressed gymnastics insiders and the media alike. It also earned praised from her coaches.

"I've never met anybody like Jo, she's always been so focused and known what she's wanted to be – the best – since she was so little," Kathryn Geddert told *ESPN*. "The Jo you see now was the same one you would have met 10 years ago. She's not going to take a break or stop until the task is accomplished."

National Team Coordinator Marta Karolyi sat in the stands watching the competition intensely. She also had high praise for the new U.S. champion.

"Jordyn proved herself," she told *USA Today*. "She is a strong person physically and mentally. I have my trust in Jordyn."

Although Jordyn had become a gymnastics superstar, she remained as down to earth as ever. She attended her older brother's high school football games and supported her younger sister who played travel soccer. The teen also spent time with her older sister Lindsay whenever she returned home from medical school at Michigan State University.

Jordyn's gymnastics prowess didn't surprise her family. She came from an athletic background. Her dad played high school baseball and football, and her mother earned a college track and field scholarship to Central Michigan University. In addition, Lindsay was a Junior Olympic National qualifier in track and field and ran in the Boston Marathon.

Right after nationals, Jordyn flew to Texas to participate in the Karolyi Camp. Run by Bela and Marta Karolyi, the legendary coaches of past champions Nadia Comaneci and Mary Lou Retton, their camp serves as the designated training site for the U.S. women's national team. For several days, gymnasts train at the facility and compete in mock competitions. At the camp's conclusion, international assignments are often handed out. It also serves as a way to build camaraderie among the elite athletes.

"I think camp helps us really bond not only in the gym but even outside," Jordyn stated. "We learn a lot more about each other and want to support each other and cheer each other on."

Due in large part to her stunning display at nationals, Jordyn earned a spot on the world team. In early October, she and her teammates arrived in Tokyo, Japan, for the 2011 World Championships.

"I think we have a really good chance [to win] if everyone competes to their potential," Jordyn remarked before the competition. "I think we have a really strong team."

Early in the week, Team USA suffered a serious loss when their team captain, Alicia Sacramone, tore her Achilles tendon. The Americans vowed to bring home the team gold medal for their injured teammate.

And they did just that, winning the team title by more than four points over second place finisher Russia. The American girls grinned proudly as they stood on the podium displaying their gold medals.

"We all wanted it so bad but we knew we couldn't let ourselves get too cocky or confident," Jordyn remarked afterwards.

"We just thought about coming in here and just doing our routines and not paying attention to who was winning."

"It's such an honor to be a part of a world championship gold medal team, and I'm so happy to be here to experience this," she added. "We just tried to do our routines but also have fun, and I think that really helped us."

Jordyn's steady performances in the team event qualified her for the all-around competition. On October 13, 2011, she marched into the crowded arena. Her face showed focus and determination as she readied for the biggest individual meet of her career.

Throughout the all-around competition, Jordyn engaged in a close battle for the top spot with Russia's Viktoria Komova. The title came down to the last apparatus, the floor exercise. A tough competitor, the American unleashed a strong routine and then waited to see what the judges would do.

"It was kind of a little bit nerve-wracking," she said. "Waiting at that point, I didn't know if my floor routine was enough to win it. I just had to wait and see what the scoreboard would tell us."

In the end, the Michigan native won the gold by a whisker of .033 points. When Jordyn learned of her victory, her mouth fell open in disbelief and she burst into joyful tears.

"It means so much to me," the emotional teen remarked. "It's a dream come true."

"It was such a happy moment," she later recalled. "I just remember seeing my name, and then all of a sudden, I'm up on the podium. I was like, 'Wow, I'm the world champion.'"

"She's going to go out there and give you 100 percent every time out," John Geddert raved to the *Associated Press*. "You can't ask for any more out of a kid or an athlete, that's for sure."

"Good things come to those who wait?" she once tweeted. "Nope…good things come to those who work their butt off and never give up."

Now a world champion, Jordyn received much attention when she returned home. Suddenly she found herself featured in newspapers, magazines and even on television.

One day Jordyn received a huge thrill when she was invited on the popular daytime talk show hosted by comedian Ellen DeGeneres. Wearing a lavender warm-up suit, the new world champion appeared poised throughout the interview. The talk show host first asked how the U.S. and world champion became involved in elite gymnastics.

"When I was about six or seven, I started practicing a lot more," Jordyn explained. "Then I started competing… Once I got out there on the stage and started competing, I loved it. I just loved the feeling of going out there and showing off."

Later Ellen grilled Jordyn about her crush on heartthrob Justin Bieber. The obsessed teen listened to his music all the time and had watched his movie over ten times. After winning worlds, she famously tweeted: "Now that we are world champions…can we meet Justin Bieber yet? #welldeserved… Who has connections!?!?"

"I figure he gets a lot of tweets already, so I don't want to bother him," she answered calmly when asked if she'd ever tweeted the singer.

Ellen also asked how it felt to compete against the other girls. Was it strange to compete against friends?

"We're so used to it," Jordyn replied. "All the U.S. girls… we train together. We're pretty much best friends, but when it gets out into competition, we don't think about beating each other. We just think about doing our own thing."

When Jordyn returned to school, classmates recognized her from TV. She also garnered interested looks when walking down the hallway. At first the attention she received at school felt strange, but soon everything died down and returned to normal.

Besides, despite her impressive resume, Jordyn remained your average teenager. When the world champion wasn't busy with school or gymnastics, she liked chatting online, shopping for clothes at Hollister and sketching. The thoughtful athlete also enjoyed reading and considered *Secrets of My Hollywood Life* her favorite book.

Now that she was world all-around champion, expectations for Jordyn skyrocketed. However, the levelheaded gymnast did not shy away from her new role as favorite.

"I don't feel too much pressure," she remarked. "I try not to think about it. I just try to stay focused on my goals and do what I know how to do which is perform my routines and just try to stay consistent."

Being a strong all-around competitor means you always train and compete all four disciplines. People often asked Jordyn to name her favorite apparatus. The answer came easily to her: balance beam.

"When you're doing new skills, it can get a little nerve-wracking," she admitted. "But I love the adrenalin rush."

With her name recognition rising each day, Jordyn used her newfound celebrity to support several charitable organizations. She volunteered at a local fundraising 5K race, worked charity projects at her church and supported St. Jude's Children's Hospital – a pediatric treatment and research facility focused on children's catastrophic diseases. It felt good to help less fortunate individuals.

The arrival of 2012 brought the long awaited Olympic season. As usual, Jordyn flew to Texas to attend the Karolyi Camp. Immediately she sensed a tense vibe among her teammates.

"Right now the atmosphere is pretty serious," she said. "We're all doing a lot of training...a lot of practicing and just trying to put all the things in our routines for the home stretch leading up to the summer. At the same time, we're really bonding as a team and having a lot of fun."

Jordyn began the Olympic year by winning American Cup for the third time. Her victory tied her with Mary Lou Retton as the only gymnast to win the competition three times.

"Worlds opened Jordyn's eyes to the fact that she really is that good," Kathryn told *ESPN*. "It was a close competition with the Russians, and it gave her confidence knowing how well she did against the best in the world."

When Jordyn arrived at the 2012 Visa Championships in St. Louis, Missouri, experts touted her as the strong favorite for the all-around title. As the final competitor on day one, she trailed Gabby Douglas in the standings and needed a strong floor routine to move up in the rankings. Her response? She delivered perhaps the best routine of her career to pull up to a dead tie with her rival.

"My coach told me the score that I needed before I went out there," the world champion revealed. "It made me want to squeeze every little tenth out of my routine."

"It felt really good to come out on top tonight," she added. "It definitely gives me a little motivation for Sunday."

Jordyn liked having a close challenger for the top spot. In fact, the feisty competitor enjoyed the battle.

"I usually thrive off the pressure, and it's so fun to have someone else so close," she told *The Associated Press*. "It's more exciting."

"It's kind of like a dogfight out there," she added. "But we're really supportive of each other, and it just shows the depth of the U.S. team."

Meanwhile, Jordyn's coaches couldn't have been more proud. In particular, John felt that his student faced a greater challenge defending a title than trying to win it for the first time.

"When you look at the history of the sport, it's a lot easier being the one chasing the rabbit, than being the rabbit," John said. "Jordyn is who she is; when she needs to pull something out, she does. We love the fight."

"There's a lot of added pressure, but she'll step it up," he continued. "This is actually good for her to know, you're not a lock for the top spot. Initial jitters are gone. It's going to be a dogfight. That's Team USA."

Jordyn and Gabby's first place battle reminded many of past epic showdowns between Nastia Liukin and Shawn Johnson. Sitting in the stands watching the competition unfold, Shawn was also reminded of her past rivalry.

"You look over and see the other one doing something new and harder, and you think, 'I have to go home and raise my difficulty,'" she told the *Los Angeles Times*.

Two days later, a focused Jordyn unleashed four solid routines. At the end of the afternoon, she successfully defended her national all-around title and also added a floor exercise silver medal to her resume.

"It feels even better to know that I won two years in a row because I've worked so hard in the gym," Jordyn remarked.

"I went 8 for 8 so I was happy with that," she added.

Jordyn wasn't just pleased with her own performance, though. She also praised her competitors.

"It's so exciting to see the depth of this U.S. team," she raved. "I'm so proud of everyone. It was a great show out there."

The intense competition would continue at Olympic Trials in San Jose, California. Already Jordyn looked forward to the event by focusing on the training that would precede it.

"There's so much I want to improve on in the next couple weeks," she stressed. "It was a great competition, but I definitely wasn't 100%. For the next two weeks, I'm going to work on the small details. I'll get in the gym and work on the consistency in my routines and make sure I get every tenth out of my routines."

With the Olympics just weeks away, interest in Jordyn intensified. Shortly after winning the 2011 World Championships, the gymnastics star had made the weighty decision to turn professional. This major move meant that she could now accept financial rewards with the knowledge that doing so would forfeit her NCAA eligibility. After twelve years of costly gymnastics lessons, it felt good to reap financial rewards from her hard work.

Several months before the London Olympics, Jordyn signed a commercial deal with the Kellogg Company. The cereal and convenience food manufacturer plastered the world champion's image on boxes of Kellogg's Corn Flakes as part of a campaign on Olympic-bound athletes. Jordyn could walk down the cereal aisle at her local grocery store and find her face staring back at her!

"I was so excited," she told the *Today Show*. "I never thought I would be on the front of a Kellogg's Corn Flakes box. It was the most surreal thing."

With the Olympics so close, people everywhere asked Jordyn about the 2012 London Games. The sixteen-year-old never took her place on the team for granted.

"Obviously to make an Olympic team is a great goal and she deserves it," John Geddert said practically. "We really want to help her get there."

"It's brutal," Rita admitted honestly. "Five girls will make the team, and there are more than five girls that are amazing."

When asked directly about her bid for the Olympic team, Jordyn had a mixture of both excitement and enthusiasm.

"I'm definitely excited," she admitted. "It's gonna be a fun journey. I'm looking forward to it."

Meanwhile, Michigan natives were also excited for Jordyn's success. In fact, the world champion inspired many children in the state to enroll in gymnastics classes. Gyms and YMCAs in the area reported up to 40% enrollment increases!

"Kids are always coming in and asking about [Jordyn], talking about her," Chris Meese of Oak Park YMCA told *WILX.com*.

"It's a rare and wonderful thing to have someone of that caliber of gymnastics come from here," Jamie Boyd-Hamilton from Red Cedar Gymnastics agreed. "I mean just to have that drive, the desire, the ability, the parent support and her body stay healthy, it's just like a miracle in our own backyard."

Jordyn also had her fair share of fans, too. Her official website enjoyed steady traffic and her *Twitter* page attracted almost 20,000 followers with admirers from all over the world. The accomplished athlete remembered how it felt to idolize gymnastics heroes.

"I had a lot of favorites," she remembered. "I liked Mary Lou Retton and Carly Patterson, and Nastia (Liukin) was always a huge role model of mine, too."

"Over the years, every Olympic team has helped the sport of gymnastics just grow even stronger," she added.

As Jordyn prepared for the 2012 Olympic Trials in San Jose, California, Wieber fever invaded DeWitt, Michigan. All over town, store owners hung signs in front of their businesses expressing their best wishes to its most famous resident.

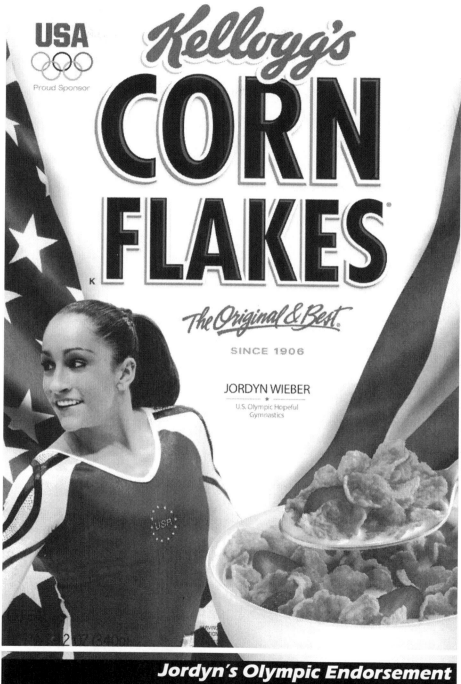

Jordyn's Olympic Endorsement
(Kellogg's)

"I'll be in the grocery store and people will come up to me and wish me good luck," Jordyn told *WILX.com*. "I can't even explain how unbelievably lucky I feel to live in this community where everyone is so supportive."

The town's goodwill extended toward the rest of the Wiebers as well. When the close-knit family wondered how they would afford to travel to London to watch Jordyn compete, various fundraisers were held to raise money for them.

As the London Olympics loomed in the near future, many asked how the world champion might mentally approach the games. The down-to-earth teen set admirable goals.

"My personal goals are basically just to have fun and enjoy it," she remarked. "After that, to do my routines to the best of my ability and make sure I don't have any regrets. Don't be timid when I'm competing and make sure I'm really confident and aggressive."

Although Jordyn loved gymnastics dearly, she set goals outside of gymnastics, too. She planned to attend college someday and considered UCLA her top school. That came as little surprise to those who knew her. She loved visiting California more than any other state.

Before the start of trials, Olympic champion Tim Daggett appeared on the *Today Show* to discuss the upcoming competition. A reporter asked him about Jordyn's chances of making the team.

"It would be hard to imagine her not being on the team," he said. "They're not going to say that she's a lock but she's a lock."

Wearing a sporty red and white leotard, Jordyn began day one of trials with a strong vault. She moved on to the uneven bars next where she delivered an outstanding routine. On her third apparatus, the balance beam, the well-conditioned athlete looked steady and confident.

"It is obvious how hard she has worked since championships," *NBC* commentator Elfi Schlegel raved. "She has just gotten better and better."

Jordyn ended night one on the floor exercise where she produced another strong performance. When the pleased gymnast came off the floor, she gave an enthusiastic high five to John. She finished the evening firmly in first place.

"I've been working so hard to try to improve at every competition," she said afterwards. "I think I've improved a lot since Visa's so I'm happy to come out and hit four strong routines."

"I have to stay focused and take it one routine at a time," she added.

"I just loved the way she went out and attacked it," John told *NBC*. "She had some issues so there's room for improvement and it's my job to point that out. I don't think we've ever had a meet where I didn't say, 'There are things to improve.' We're still waiting for the perfect meet."

On night two of the competition, Jordyn faced the uneven bars first and gave another strong routine. The crowd responded with huge applause. The sixteen-year-old competed on the balance beam next, and though she committed a few small bobbles and balance checks, it was a successful performance.

"She looks absolutely unstoppable," raved Tim.

Jordyn performed her popular floor routine next, wowing the crowd with her powerful tumbling and energetic dance moves. For her final rotation, she executed a strong Amanar vault.

With her work behind her, Jordyn would have to wait and see if the three-person committee would select her for the Olympic team. The nervous teen sat backstage with the other gymnasts and waited for news. After what seemed like an eternity, Marta Karolyi finally entered the room and announced the 2012 Olympic gymnastics team.

Gabby Douglas

McKayla Maroney

Aly Raisman

Kyla Ross

Jordyn Wieber

She had done it! The girl from DeWitt, Michigan, could pack her bags for London!

Jordyn immediately began shedding tears of happiness and relief. After so many years of waiting and wanting, she was officially an Olympian.

"I was just so happy," she recalled. "I know how much hard work it took each and everyone of us to get here. To finally hear my name called...it's the best day of my life."

Moments later, Jordyn stood in front of 17,000 screaming fans as she and her teammates were introduced as members of the 2012 Olympic team. Her eyes puffy and red, she waved triumphantly to the crowd, wiped away more tears and shook her head in disbelief.

"It's more emotional than I thought it would be," she said afterwards. "I'm just so happy and honored that I'll be representing USA in London."

Once Jordyn had officially been named to the team, gymnastics enthusiasts began speculating on her medal chances in London. Could she lead the American girls to a team victory? Would the world champion become the third straight American woman to claim all-around gold?

Regardless of how Jordyn performs in London, one thing remains certain. She will always cherish her gymnastics experiences.

"It's just been so much fun and such a great experience not only just the gymnastics part but just being able to travel everywhere and meet tons of great people," Jordyn gushed. "It's just been the experience of a lifetime. I'm so happy I'm a gymnast."

Competitive Record

National Results

2012 Olympic Trials
2nd-All-Around, Floor Exercise; 3rd-Balance Beam

2012 Visa Championships
1st-All-Around; 2nd-Floor Exercise

2012 Secret U.S. Classic
1st-Balance Beam

2011 Visa Championships
1st-All-Around, Uneven Bars, Floor Exercise; 3rd-Balance Beam

2011 CoverGirl Classic
1st-Uneven Bars, Balance Beam

2010 CoverGirl Classic
1st-All-Around, Vault, Uneven Bars; 2nd-Floor Exercise (Jr. Div.)

2008 Visa Championships
1st-All-Around, Vault, Floor Exercise; 2nd-Balance Beam; 3rd-Uneven Bars (Jr. Div.)

2008 U.S. Classic
1st-All-Around, Vault, Uneven Bars, Balance Beam, Floor Exercise (Jr. Div.)

2007 Visa Championships
2nd-Vault, Balance Beam; 3rd-All-Around, Uneven Bars (Jr. Div.)

2007 U.S. Classic
2nd-Balance Beam, Vault; 5th-All-Around (Jr. Div.)

2006 Visa Championships
9th-All-Around (Jr. Div.)

2006 U.S. Classic
10th-All-Around (Jr. Div.)

International Results

2012 Kellogg's Pacific Rim Championships
1st-Team, All-Around, Floor Exercise

2012 AT&T American Cup
1st-All-Around

2011 World Championships
1st-Team, All-Around; 3rd-Balance Beam

2011 City of Jesolo Trophy
1st-Team; 2nd-All-Around, Vault, Balance Beam; 3rd-Uneven Bars

2011 AT&T American Cup
1st-All-Around

2010 Pacific Rim Championships
1st-Team, All-Around, Uneven Bars, Floor Exercise; 2nd-Vault (Jr. Div.)

2009 Junior Team Cup of International Gymnix
1st-Team, All-Around, Vault, Uneven Bars, Balance Beam, Floor Exercise

2009 Tyson American Cup
1st-All-Around

2008 Top Gym
1st-All-Around

2008 Italy-Spain-Poland-USA Competition
1st-Team, All-Around (Jr. Div.)

2007 Junior Pan American Championships
1st-Team, Uneven Bars, Balance Beam; 2nd-All-Around; 3rd-Floor Exercise

"I want to inspire people. Like, 'if Gabby can do it then I can do it.'"

"THE FLYING SQUIRREL"

On December 31,1995, festive partygoers celebrated New Year's Eve. Adults popped champagne, smitten sweethearts kissed and youngsters blew noisemakers. When the clock struck twelve, "Happy New Year!" echoed throughout the country.

Meanwhile, in a Virginia Beach hospital room, a young mother named Natalie lovingly cradled her newborn daughter. She named her baby Gabrielle, which means "God is my strength." Little "Brie" had three older siblings: Johnathan, Joyelle and Arie.

Several years later, Arie began taking a gymnastics class. The young girl loved the energetic tumbling. One day while practicing, she taught a cartwheel to two-year-old Gabby. The toddler mimicked the move flawlessly with perfectly straight legs.

Arie stopped in her tracks. Had she seen correctly?

"Do the cartwheel again," she urged her younger sister.

Gabby didn't blink as she executed another perfect cartwheel.

"Mom, come here," Arie called excitedly. "Look at Gabby's great cartwheels!"

Natalie watched carefully as her tiny daughter unleashed another textbook cartwheel. Sure, Gabby's talent impressed the hardworking single mother, but Mom didn't exactly jump for joy. Only months earlier, Arie broke her wrist doing backhand springs. Did she want another daughter breaking her delicate bones? No thanks.

As the weeks passed, Arie ran home from gymnastics class each afternoon and taught that day's lesson to her younger sister. Little Gabby never flinched from the difficult skills, performing them with grace and astonishing flexibility. Soon the toddler learned one-handed cartwheels and the splits.

Natalie finally relented and enrolled her four children in a trial gymnastics class. Joy and John quickly expressed disinterest and dropped out of the class.

When Gabby first entered the gym, her expressive brown eyes focused on a large trampoline dominating the room. A bashful smile filled her angelic face.

"Can I jump on that?" she whispered.

When the budding gymnast climbed onto the resilient springboard, she hopped, flipped and giggled for several blissful minutes until her turn ended. Then she looked hopefully at her coach and asked sweetly, "Can I go again?"

Before long, though, Gabby sampled the other apparatuses and loved them all. The floor exercise let her become a tumbling ballerina, while the uneven bars favored power and strength. The vault let her fly, and the balance beam suited her flexibility and impeccable balance.

Gymnastics enthralled Gabby. She grinned constantly. One day her coaches erupted into giggles as they watched the small gymnast dart down the vault runway sporting a big smile. Most gymnasts looked terrified as they sped toward the difficult apparatus, but Gabby couldn't stop smiling!

The years passed quickly as Gabby rocketed up the competitive ranks mastering tricky skills at a surprisingly swift rate. On some Saturday mornings, she proudly slipped on a glittery leotard and competed for her gym. The exhilaration of competition, the apparatuses, the crowds, the scores, the medals... Gabby loved every aspect of gymnastics.

During the summer of 2004, eight-year-old Gabby sat wide-eyed in front of the television watching athletes from all over the world compete for their country. From the spectacular opening ceremonies to thrilling sports coverage to the closing ceremonies, she loved every second of the Athens Summer Olympics.

Gabby especially adored the gymnastics all-around competition, where the top girls competed on all four apparatuses. At the conclusion of the competition, the gymnast with the highest overall total won the gold medal. Because the all-around event requires athletes to show strength in every discipline, it's considered the most difficult and prestigious title.

An epic showdown occurred during the Athens' all-around championship. Legendary Svetlana Khorkina from Russia, competing in her final Olympics, made one final bid for the all-around title that she'd missed in two previous games. Many considered the graceful twenty-five-year-old one of the most artistic gymnasts ever. Meanwhile, the United States rested their hopes on Carly Patterson, a tiny teenager with ex-

The Flying Squirrel
(Anthony L. Solis)

plosive gymnastics. The gymnasts, polar opposites in both style and personality, created a truly memorable competition.

In the end, the bubbly Louisiana native became the first American woman to win the all-around in a fully attended Olympics. Her victory inspired a new generation of young gymnasts, including Gabby Douglas. After watching Carly's Athens' victory, the tiny athlete began daydreaming about her own Olympics. Could she follow Carly's example by one day competing on sports' biggest stage?

Gabby now trained in her hometown at Excalibur Gymnastics in Virginia Beach, Virginia. In May of 2008, she qualified for the Level 10 Championships in Orlando, Florida. The Douglas clan attended the competition, turning it into a vacation as well. They visited Walt Disney World and Universal Studios, creating a memorable outing for all!

Later that year, Gabby became an elite gymnast. The twelve-year-old competed as a junior at the 2008 Visa Championships in Boston, Massachusetts, and placed 16th in the all-around. After the competition ended, she and her family explored the historic city.

Gabby also attended the senior championships. She watched wide-eyed as Olympic-bound athletes Shawn Johnson, Nastia Liukin and Alicia Sacramone performed routines they would also compete in Beijing. She idolized the formidable trio and wondered if she might some day also chase an Olympic dream.

Later Gabby watched on television as the American gymnastics team competed in the Beijing Olympics. Although she cheered for all the girls, one gymnast especially captivated her.

"Watching Shawn in Beijing, she was so perfect," she later recalled. "Every skill she did was finished. Bam! She stuck it! The crowd went wild. To see that happen, it amazed me."

The gymnastics competition excited little Gabby so much that she ran around her house in an animated frenzy. The youngster could barely contain her excitement.

"Mom! Mom! Did you see that?" she shrieked. "Look! Look! Look! Maybe I could do that one day!"

Gabby's talent didn't surprise Natalie. All her children were athletic. Arielle liked ballroom dancing, and Joelle adored figure skating. Meanwhile, Johnathan enjoyed football, track and martial arts.

The following year, the junior gymnast dealt with a serious injury. Although she traveled to Dallas, Texas, for the 2009

Visa Championships, she competed only on the balance beam and placed a respectable 5th.

When Gabby arrived in Hartford, Connecticut, for the 2010 Visa Championships, she felt healthy and confident. Those positive qualities helped her nab 4th in the junior all-around and a balance beam silver medal.

Although Gabby had achieved steady results, she possessed even loftier ambition. She dreamed of winning national titles and soaring on world and Olympic stages. To achieve such goals, she needed a coaching change.

"I told my mom, 'I really want to make my dream come alive,'" she later recalled. "'I want to make it happen.'"

The determined gymnast believed one man could guide her: Liang Chow. The popular coach with a great reputation owned a gym in West Des Moines, Iowa. He'd coached Shawn Johnson to a world all-around title and four Olympic medals, including balance beam gold. His gymnasts produced top results, but they also had fun.

Gabby met Chow years earlier at a camp and instantly liked him. Meanwhile, the teenager's drive and determination had impressed the former Chinese competitor.

After much thought, Gabby asked her mother for permission to move to the Midwest and train under Chow. Although Natalie would miss her daughter greatly, she agreed to support her daughter's dream. When the ambitious athlete contacted Chow about coaching her, he admired her courage.

"I give her a lot of credit for having the guts to pursue her ambition," he said.

So in February of 2011, Gabby moved to West Des Moines, Iowa. Immediately upon her arrival, the teen felt certain she'd made the correct decision.

"When I came to Chow's, everyone was just so loving and, 'Hey, you're the new girl, and we made you this casserole,' she revealed to *USA Today*. "Everyone was just so caring and I just loved it, and I love being there."

Chow helped Gabby find a new home with a host family. Travis and Missy Parton had contacted him months earlier and offered housing to any athlete who needed it. They were the parents of four girls and happy to welcome a fifth one. Fortunately for all involved, Gabby and the Partons adored each other.

"I'm like a big sister," she remarked happily. "I really like it."

On many evenings, Gabby and her "sisters" played Xbox 360 Kinect. Sometimes they microwaved popcorn, rented a movie and played nail salon. One afternoon they attended the Iowa State Fair.

In particular, Gabby grew closest to the youngest Parton child. She even taught the young girl certain gymnastics skills. Her tiny fan felt thrilled to have a world-class gymnast for her personal coach!

"The determination that she has, leaving her family at 14 years old to move to a different city," Missy Parton told the *Des Moines Register*. "I'm just so amazed by her, and we're so proud of her."

Big changes highlighted 2011. Gabby graduated into the senior ranks and could now compete at worlds and the Olympics. The focused athlete surrounded herself with motivational thoughts–literally. She wrote inspirational sentences on a whiteboard in her bedroom. The positive thoughts served as constant reminders of her enormous goals. Quotes included: "I refuse to quit" and "I refuse to give up!"

Gabby also began her sophomore year of high school. Due to her busy schedule, she took online courses. The hardworking fifteen-year-old enjoyed several classes with history as her favorite.

Working with Chow immediately benefitted Gabby's gymnastics. Her consistency increased and she acquired several new skills. Plus, the sport became fun again. She laughed and smiled more than ever.

Around the same time, Chow's former student, Shawn Johnson, announced a comeback attempt for the 2012 London Olympics. Suddenly, Gabby had a training mate. Working beside an Olympic champion every day proved humbling and motivating for the teenager.

"Shawn's so inspirational," Gabby told *USA Gymnastics*. "She's coming back from all her injuries and dealing with so much. I love training with her."

"The move has definitely paid off," she added. "Everyone tells me I'm a new person and I'm a new gymnast."

Whenever Gabby felt overwhelmingly homesick, she called, texted or emailed her mom. Meanwhile, her father was stationed in Afghanistan on his third tour of duty with the

Air Force. Although Gabby missed him dearly, she wrote him regularly.

"It makes me feel so honored and proud that he's my dad," she declared.

When the 2011 Visa Championships arrived, Gabby grappled with a leg injury that limited her training. It wasn't an ideal way to begin her senior career. On the first day of competition, the frustrated gymnast committed several mistakes in her routines and lingered in 12th place.

Gabby's family made the 12-hour drive to St. Paul, Minnesota, to watch her compete. When the close-knit group returned to their hotel room, the despondent athlete sat quietly while her mother wrapped her leg with ice. Natalie then opened her laptop and searched for her daughter's finest routines on *YouTube*. As Gabby's eyes grew heavy, her mother offered terrific advice.

"Today is behind you, so leave it there," Natalie recounted on her blog, *Brie and her Big Cheese*. "Tomorrow is standing before you - focus on that."

Buoyed by the pep talk, Gabby rebounded strongly on day two. She sprang up to seventh in the all-around and snatched a bronze medal on the uneven bars.

Shortly after nationals, Gabby flew to Huntsville, Texas, for camp where Marta Karolyi would evaluate national competitors and name the world team. The rejuvenated gymnast felt fit and focused.

"I was doing a lot of numbers in training in the gym, trying to boost up my self-confidence and my consistency," she told *USA Gymnastics*. "I went into camp focused, knowing I'm going to hit my routines at the right moment when it counts."

Upon the camp's conclusion, Marta gathered the girls and announced the world team. Among the prestigious group? Gabby Douglas! Her teammates included: Jordyn Wieber, Alicia Sacramone, Sabrina Vega, McKayla Maroney and Aly Raisman.

In early October, Gabby flew to Tokyo, Japan, for the 2012 World Gymnastics Championships. The chipper teen embraced the time change and foreign cuisine.

"I like the time zone and getting up earlier and chilling," she explained enthusiastically. "I love the food. The rice is really good."

The team competition marked the championships' first event. Unfortunately, before the event got underway, Team USA captain Alicia Sacramone tore her Achilles tendon. The remaining American girls vowed to win the gold medal for their fallen teammate.

In the end, the U.S. girls dominated the competition, winning the team title by more than four points over second place finisher Russia. Meanwhile, China finished a distant third. For the rest of her life, Gabby would be called a world champion!

Thanks to a strong performance in the team event, Gabby also qualified for the bars final. In a tough field, she placed a respectable fifth.

"I could have done a little bit better connecting my skills," she analyzed. "Overall, I'm pretty satisfied being here and getting the excellent experience. I really love being here."

When Gabby landed back in Des Moines, she received a hero's welcome. Her Chow's Gymnastics teammates showered her with congratulatory signs and flowers.

"Coming down here and seeing all of Chow's team made me very happy," the flattered teen smiled.

"The whole experience was awesome," she added. "I loved representing USA. It was such an honor."

Gabby's worlds' success only increased her confidence and drive. The youngster finally believed she could compete with gymnastics' best. Now that she tasted success, she craved it more!

The all-important 2012 Olympic season began with the AT&T American Cup at Madison Square Garden in New York. Wearing a pretty lavender leotard, Gabby entered the competition as an alternate meaning she competed in exhibition mode only. Though the judges scored her routines, she would not factor into the final standings.

Gabby performed four breathtaking routines before 12,000 screaming fans. She executed a difficult Amanar vault, impressed with a powerful bars routine and displayed elegant beam and floor exercises. Her final score of 61.299 eclipsed every competitor's marks. However, since she was not officially on the roster, she did not receive credit for the victory. Nevertheless, Gabby made a huge statement with her performances.

"I wanted to show the crowd what I'm capable of," she remarked afterwards. "I've come a long way from 2011 Worlds. My confidence level is higher."

Two weeks later, Gabby competed in Kellogg's Pacific Rim Championships, where her beautiful bars routine earned a gold medal. Meanwhile, thanks to her stunning high release skills on the apparatus, Gabby earned the nifty nickname: the Flying Squirrel. The moniker took her by surprise.

"I don't really notice it until people are like, 'Oh my God, did you see how high you were?'..." she told *USA Today*. "It doesn't really feel that way. It never really feels like how it looks."

"I love the nickname," she smiled. "It shows my potential on the bars, whether it's my release moves, or my turns, or my tumbling passes. I've grown to like the Flying Squirrel."

Gabby's family members loved her nickname, too. They even created flying squirrel shirts to show their support.

In the meantime, when Gabby craved a break from school or gymnastics, she gravitated toward relaxing activities. In particular, the teenager enjoyed crocheting.

"It soothes the body and helps me relax, takes my mind off of things," she told *USA Today*. "Me and my sister were crocheting these scarves and these blankets and these hats and these baby booties. We were donating them to people who didn't have clothes. We felt so good we actually made stuff and just donated it."

Gabby also enjoyed tastes typical of a teenager. She particularly liked the *Twilight* book series. Her favorite television show? *The Vampire Diaries*. She also listened repeatedly to Rihanna, Beyonce and Adele on her iPod.

In early June, Gabby flew to St. Louis, Missouri, to compete in the 2012 Visa Championships. The confident teen strove to prove herself as a strong candidate for the Olympic team.

"I have my mental confidence up," she told *USA Today*. "I want to show what I'm capable of doing."

"She has every reason to be confident in herself," Chow agreed. "This is the year for the Olympics. We've got nothing to lose, but showing her strength, showing her gracefulness, showing her fans what she can deliver. I have belief in her."

On the competition's first day, Gabby kicked off the meet on her best event, the uneven bars. She delivered a tremendous performance.

"This is an area where Gabby would contribute hugely to Team USA," raved *NBC* announcer Elfi Schlegel. "She is unbelievable on this apparatus. Look at these release skills and exquisite form."

Gabby marched to the balance beam next. Under intense scrutiny, she delivered another solid performance. The driven athlete looked sharp and well conditioned.

"If she does everything that she's capable of, I think she can win this competition," claimed 1984 Olympic Champion Tim Daggett.

The floor exercise marked Gabby's third event of the competition. Once again she executed a clean program.

"A very strong routine for Gabby," Tim raved. "So far three times up, three times hits."

Gabby ended the evening on the vault. On this particular apparatus, the nimble gymnast performed an Amanar, which consists of 2½ twists. She broke into a huge grin when she landed it.

At the competition's midway point, Gabby boasted a big score of 60.650. Meanwhile, Jordyn Wieber also netted the same total. The two girls tied for first place!

"I feel really awesome right now," Gabby told *USA Gymnastics*. "All of my hard work has paid off. I have to keep focusing on my training and the final day of competition."

"I have this mentality that I'm a winner," she continued. "I'm going into war. This is a battle, and I've got to fight for this. . .for myself. . .for my coaches. I went out there and showed everyone what I was capable of doing."

"She shows her good gymnastics skills, but also the management of her mind was a beautiful performance," Chow told the *Des Moines Register*.

Unfortunately for Gabby, two days later, a fluke balance beam fall cost her the national title. However, she rebounded from the early mistake to deliver strong uneven bars, floor exercise and vault routines.

"Switching over your mindset of being disappointed to trying to erase and starting with a clean slate was important," Gabby told *USA Today*.

In the end, she won the all-around silver medal, missing the gold by .2 points. She also scored a floor exercise bronze medal and nabbed gold on bars.

"I was determined I was going to make the bars routine the best that I could," she said happily. "When I finished my dismount, I was so happy."

"I think competition went really well this week," she continued. "My performance today is motivating me to go to the Olympic Trials in San Jose with a fire and determination to do even better."

"She has a special lightness and freedom in the routine," Marta told *Mercury News*. "Some people may have higher difficulty values, but Gabby's execution is the best in the world."

Thanks to her exciting face off with Jordyn, people chattered excitedly about their rivalry. Their competitiveness reminded many of Nastia Liukin and Shawn Johnson's past matchups.

"We push each other to do better and greater things, like sticking every pass on the floor routine, and sticking a double pike even though you've never stuck a double pike before," Gabby told *USA Today*. "It pushes us to do awesome and greater and beautiful gymnastics."

"We're really friendly, and I feel like we're all sisters off the floor," she added "But when we're on the floor, it's rivalry, it's competitors. It's, 'This is my time to shine and I'm coming for you.' You know, that mentality on the floor."

"It's really exciting just to know it's kind of a dogfight," Jordyn agreed. "But at the same time we're real supportive of each other. And it really shows the depth of the U.S. team."

When Gabby returned to Iowa, she and Chow began training for Olympic Trials, where the London team would be announced. The hardworking duo focused on producing clean routines with as few deductions as possible. Before long it was time to leave for the competition.

The rules for the 2012 Olympic Trials stated that only the first place finisher won a spot on the London team. A committee led by Marta Karolyi would select the remaining four gymnasts immediately following the competition. Not wanting to leave anything to chance, Gabby set her sights on earning her spot with a victory.

"She could win these trials," Elfi remarked before the event. "As talented as this young lady is, her greatest challenge is to stay focused and to keep her head in the game, but don't count her out. She is a super talent."

Sporting a sparkly pink and black leotard, Gabby entered the HP Pavilion on the first night of competition feeling more excited than nervous. She scanned the crowd and grinned widely when she spotted some fans waving signs with her name on it. Later on, she laughed appreciatively when an admirer tossed her a stuffed squirrel.

As she began warming up, a man's voice called her name. When the teenager looked up, she spotted her dad in the stands. Back in the United States after six months in Afghanistan, her proud father beamed as he waved a U.S. flag that read: "Go Gabby Douglas, Love, Dad."

Gabby & Coach Chow
(AP)

An emotional Gabby felt overwhelmed. She smiled widely, swallowed hard and blinked back tears.

"Seeing him made my night, actually," the Olympic hopeful later remarked.

Her father also struggled to control his emotions. After all, he hadn't seen his daughter since 2010.

"There's an exuberance. There's a feeling that you can't describe," he told *The Des Moines Register*. "Sometimes, when she had a rough time, I'd tell her to hang in there. 'You know what it takes to be a winner, you know what your goals are. You just keep on your goals.' Some things that I tell her I have to remind myself. Those are all things we can all abide by."

As the sixteen-year-old began the competition on the uneven bars, Shawn Johnson, who ended her comeback attempt weeks earlier, sat in the stands cheering her on. Although Gabby experienced a small hiccup in her routine, she still performed strongly. On her next event, the balance beam, she delivered a solid routine. She faced the floor exercise during the third round and received the loudest ovation of the night for her infectiously fun performance. Finally, she ended the night with a strong Amanar for a second place finish.

"Man, I felt the energy from everyone and the crowd," she raved enthusiastically afterwards. "I felt so confident and great."

"I do want the top spot very badly but I'm trying not to think about first," Gabby told *NBC*. "I need to think about polishing up my skills."

When asked about being the crowd favorite, the teenager lit up. She loved making others happy through her lively performances.

"I love to perform," she smiled. "When you perform, the judges love it. Give everyone a good show to watch."

With a sharp day one behind her, Gabby was halfway toward a coveted Olympic berth. Could she hold it together for four more routines on Sunday?

"The most important thing is to believe in yourself and know that you can do it," she always told herself. She remembered her own advice and vowed to follow it.

Two nights later, wearing a deep blue leotard as dazzling as her smile, Gabby began the competition on the vault. Although she nearly fell on the Amanar in her final warm-up, the headstrong competitor nailed it when it counted for an impressive 16.0. Her outstanding effort moved her into first place.

On her second event, the uneven bars, the tenacious gymnast competed spectacularly with unbelievably high release skills. Her performance garnered a standing ovation from gymnastics coach Bela Karolyi. The sports legend knew a thing or two about amazing routines. After all, he guided Nadia Comaneci and Mary Lou Retton to all-around victories at the Olympics!

Gabby faced the balance beam for rotation three. At the beginning of the routine, she experienced some bobbles and balance checks. Doubt started to set in. "You are not coming off this beam," she told herself. The stern command worked and she quickly regrouped. The resolute athlete stayed on the apparatus and maintained her first place standing.

Only the floor exercise stood between Gabby and London. As it turned out, she gave a commanding performance with explosive tumbling. When the strong-willed athlete ended her routine, she broke into a big smile that seemed to border on relief and exhilaration.

Gabby then paced anxiously on the sidelines and waited for officials to post her score. Had she done enough to keep the lead? Suddenly she heard a fan in the stands utter three wonderful words: "Gabby, you won." She looked up at the scoreboard. First place. She had done it. She had snatched the one guaranteed Olympic spot.

One of the first to congratulate the official Olympian? Jordyn Wieber.

"Congratulations, Gabby," her rival said sincerely as she hugged her.

"Oh my gosh! I just give all the glory to God," Gabby exclaimed afterwards to an *NBC* reporter. "He's blessed me so much."

Moments later Gabby wept as she and her four teammates marched onto the floor while USA Gymnastics President Steve Penny announced them as the newest Olympians. Thousands cheered as the London-bound athletes waved to the crowd. As confetti rained from the sky, the five emotional gymnasts wiped away happy tears and embraced one another. Whatever happened in London, the "sisters" would share a bond for the rest of their lives.

As the celebration died down, reporters clamored to interview Gabby Douglas: U.S. Olympian. As usual, the good-natured gymnast was entertaining the media with her lighthearted demeanor. First, she performed a happy dance for *NBC* cameras that she called "the Dougie." Then when someone asked Gabby what she wanted to achieve in London, she responded with her trademark wit.

"Hopefully, I can catch some accents from them because I've always wanted an accent," she answered.

And a gold souvenir would be nice, too.

Kellogg's Tour Poster
(Kellogg's)

Competitive Record

National Results

2012 U.S. Olympic Trials
1st-All-Around, Uneven Bars; 3rd-Floor Exercise

2012 Visa Championships
1st-Uneven Bars; 2nd-All-Around; 3rd-Floor Exercise

2012 Secret U.S. Classic
1st-Uneven Bars; 3rd-Floor Exercise

2011 Visa Championships
3rd-Uneven Bars; 7th-All-Around

2011 CoverGirl Classic
2nd-Uneven Bars

2010 Visa Championships
2nd-Balance Beam; 4th-All-Around, Vault (Jr. Div.)

2010 CoverGirl Classic
3rd-Balance Beam; 9th-All-Around (Jr. Div.)

2010 Nastia Liukin Supergirl Cup
4th-All-Around

International Results

2012 Kellogg's Pacific Rim Championships
1st-Team, Uneven Bars

2011 World Championships
1st-Team

2011 City of Jesolo Trophy
1st-Team; 2nd-Floor Exercise; 3rd-Balance Beam; 4th-All-Around

2010 Pan American Championships
1st-Team, Uneven Bars; 5th-All-Around

"Remember to believe in yourself. You're only at the competition, or wherever you are, because of how hard you've worked."

"TARZAN"

On December 9, 1995, in a Southern California hospital, Michael and Erin Maroney became the proud parents of a beautiful little girl. They named their daughter McKayla Rose, which means, "Who is like God?" Many years later, they welcomed two more children, Tarynn and Kav, to their blessed lives.

The daughter of a former Purdue quarterback, McKayla lived up to her athletic pedigree very quickly. When the young girl turned two years old, she watched the movie *Tarzan*. Suddenly, she began imitating the famous character by walking on her hands and legs.

"We'd be in the grocery store and I'd be asking her to walk upright, please," Erin recalled to the *Los Angeles Times*.

Like most parents, Michael and Erin assumed their child would eventually tire of her role-playing. Yet McKayla displayed an attention span and commitment far greater than most children. The focused toddler proceeded to walk like Tarzan for two years!

Little McKayla also possessed an unbelievably active streak. No matter how much she ran, crawled or played, she never seemed to tire, leaving her parents exhausted. Then one day, inspiration hit Erin. Gymnastics! Perhaps tumbling would utilize her daughter's unrelenting energy?

Several weeks later, Erin delivered McKayla to a gymnastics class in Orange County. The young girl's bright eyes sparkled with delight as she watched soaring gymnasts dance and fly around the gym.

Right off the bat, McKayla displayed a special talent on the vault, the apparatus that would one day bring her international fame and success. However, she also loved working on the balance beam and uneven bars. Plus, the floor exercise's tumbling and dance elements brought her much joy, too. In short, she loved every aspect of gymnastics.

"She was happiest in the gym," Erin recalled to *The Orange County Register*. "When she walks in the gym there's a feeling that comes over. It completes her."

While at the gym, McKayla met a talented young gymnast named Kyla Ross. The girls quickly forged a meaningful friendship after discovering that they shared the same goals and dreams. They remained good friends as they advanced quickly up the ranks.

As the years passed, McKayla fell deeper and deeper in love with gymnastics. Soon she spent several hours a day at the gym polishing new skills.

"It was always my choice to do gymnastics," she later recalled. "I always wanted to be in the gym. It's always been my dream and my goal."

If McKayla had a morning lesson, she always set her alarm clock. She would then beg her mother for a ride to the gym, so she could squeeze in a training session.

"Mom, I need to leave now," she would implore impatiently. "I have to get to practice!"

In the summer of 2004, McKayla watched the Athens Olympics on television. Although she found qualities to admire in all the gymnasts, she particularly liked American Carly Patterson whose explosive gymnastics won a gold and two silver medals at those games.

"I remember watching Carly Patterson stick her Double Arabian beam dismount," she recalled. "I just remember being like, 'Oh my gosh, I want to be there and I want to be one of them. I want to be a gymnast on the Olympic team.' That's kind of when my dreams started."

Meanwhile, the budding gymnast began competing, too. She spent many weekends partaking in club meets. The intense youngster loved the adrenalin rush that accompanied competition and the roar of the crowd when she nailed an element.

While Michael certainly understood the lure of competitive sports, he knew very little about gymnastics, which suited his daughter just fine. She liked the idea of having a sport all to herself. So rather than offering his daughter specific advice, McKayla's father always urged her to do her best and have fun.

Like many young gymnasts, McKayla began to formulate Olympic dreams as her career progressed. However, the dedicated athlete also took great satisfaction in simply learning new skills and perfecting them. As a result, this approach led to her having strong technique on all the disciplines.

Despite being a gymnastics prodigy, McKayla still enjoyed other physical activities. The adventurous youngster

McKayla Vaults to Gold
(Samantha Crawford)

often explored the neighborhood on her shiny pink bike. She also dabbled in soccer, tennis and ice skating.

In the summer of 2009, McKayla trained at Costa Mesa's Gym-Max Academy of Gymnastics. The junior-level gymnast felt thrilled when she qualified for the Visa Championships in Dallas, Texas. When she left the competition, she had nabbed a bronze medal in the vault event.

McKayla then made a major change during the off-season. She began training in Los Angeles at the All Olympia Gymnastics Center. 1980 Olympian Galina Marinova and former Soviet competitor Artur Akopyan became her new coaches.

"I'm really loving it," she gushed to *The Examiner*. "The coaches are great. I love it there."

"Galina has helped me so much with the dance and Artur with the technique, so I feel like I've gotten a lot better," she added.

As a competitive athlete, McKayla treated her body with great care. The sensible teenager paid close attention to proper nutrition. She ate the right foods to give her energy for training while also keeping her trim.

"I like to eat healthy foods so that I can get enough energy for the day," she told *Teen Vogue*. "I start my day with cereal, eggs, fruit or oatmeal, and I like chicken, salads, pasta, fruits and vegetables. Portions are important: you can eat healthily, but it matters how much you eat."

Around the same time, McKayla began receiving much attention and praise for her stellar vaulting ability. In particular, people raved over her execution of the Amanar vault, a difficult maneuver that required two and a half twists. Although other girls also did the vault, no one performed it as beautifully as McKayla could. Not only did the extraordinary vaulter boast beautiful form, she got huge height on it, too.

"It's definitely the closest thing to flying," she stated. "It's very technical. You have to be doing the right thing at the right time. It comes naturally because you've done it so many times. It's the best feeling, especially when you know that it's going to be a good vault."

When McKayla arrived in Hartford, Connecticut, to compete as a junior at the 2010 Visa Championships, she hoped to improve her previous year's placements. She reached her goal by winning the vault gold medal and finishing third in the all-around. In an impressive showing, her vault victory would have won her the senior title, too.

Following nationals, USA Gymnastics selected McKayla to compete at the 2010 Pan American Championships in Guadalajara, Mexico. At the prestigious competition, the determined gymnast and her five teammates won the team event by nearly 20 points over their nearest competitor! McKayla also won vault and floor exercise gold medals. She cherished the privilege to represent her country.

"Competing for USA is always a great honor because I'm doing something that I've always dreamed of, and I'm doing it for my country," she told *USA Gymnastics*.

With the arrival of the 2011 season, McKayla became a senior gymnast. Although many competitors considered it a huge transition, the composed athlete shrugged off any pressure.

"It's no different for any gymnast," she claimed. "You're still going to compete. It's probably more fun to know you're getting ready for the Olympics. If anything, it's more exciting."

In mid-March, McKayla traveled to Italy for the City of Jesolo Trophy and felt pleased to room with her good friend Gabby Douglas. Something that didn't please her? The beds in Italy. They were too hard and tiny!

The American girls performed beautifully and earned a decisive team victory. Meanwhile, McKayla won all-around and vault gold medals! When the competition ended, the girls celebrated with a well-deserved trip to Venice.

"It was one of the most beautiful places I have ever been," McKayla raved. "The whole time I was there I felt like I was in a movie. We went shopping, rode on the gondolas, and did all of the stuff that tourists would do. It was so much fun and I would definitely love to go there again."

"It was a gorgeous country with great people," she added. "It was an experience of a lifetime."

Despite traveling all over the world, homeschooled McKayla always kept up her studies. Her favorite subject? English. A ferocious reader, she counted *Audrey, Wait!, Tuck Everlasting, The Last Song, A Dog's Life* and *The Mysterious Benedict Society* as her favorite books. She also enjoyed series novels like *The Hunger Games, Uglies* and *Percy Jackson.*

Music also played an influential role in McKayla's life. She cited floor exercise as her favorite event because it allowed her to express herself. Her favorite musical artists included: Nicki Minaj, Taylor Swift, Rihanna and Justin Bieber.

St. Paul, Minnesota, played host for the 2011 Visa Championships. At her first senior nationals, McKayla struggled on the competition's first night. On day two, however, she shot up to second in the all-around and won the vault title.

"I just had to keep really aggressive and forget about it and move on and do the best I could on the second day," she revealed.

After McKayla proved herself at nationals and a selection camp, USA Gymnastics named her to the 2011 world team. Her other teammates included good friends, Jordyn Wieber and Aly Raisman. Meanwhile, Gabby Douglas, Alicia Sacramone and Sabrina Vega rounded out the roster.

McKayla arrived in Tokyo, Japan, in early October for the biggest competition of her life, the 2011 World Gymnastics Championships. On the first day of podium training, the American girls worked through some early jitters to deliver strong practice routines.

"It was really fun," McKayla commented afterwards. "I thought it was going to be a little bit scary but everything went really well. All the girls did awesome today."

When the actual competition began, the American girls proved unstoppable and won team gold in dominating fashion. A valuable team member, McKayla posted the competition's highest individual score with 16.033 on vault.

Needless to say, McKayla easily qualified for vault finals. Before the event, teammate Alicia Sacramone, who withdrew from worlds after she ruptured her Achilles tendon, urged her to be aggressive and win the title for the United States.

In the end, McKayla performed two spectacular vaults to win the gold medal by almost half a point over the second place finisher. The fifteen-year-old was now a two-time world champion!

"I was really calm," she told the *Los Angeles Times*. "I didn't worry. I just felt really good going out there."

"It was really fun to be out there and to be in vault finals," she added. "I did a good vault, and I got the gold medal so I'm really happy with everything."

"She was really electrifying," USA Gymnastics President Steve Penny raved. "Members of the technical committee said they were impressed by every one of her vaults."

Meanwhile, Alicia used her *Twitter* account to congratulate the new vault champion.

"So proud you kept it in the country!" she tweeted. "That's my girl!"

When McKayla returned home to Southern California, she celebrated Halloween with a good friend. The pair dressed as M&Ms and trick or treated around their neighborhood.

Despite her hectic schedule, McKayla always found the time to socialize with friends. Her favorite activities included: going to the movies, lounging at the beach or pool and shopping at the local mall.

Now a two-time world champion, budding gymnasts looked to McKayla for inspiration. Many asked her to reveal her secret for how she controlled her nerves so well. After all, she always appeared calm and collected even under the most stressful circumstances.

"I do get nervous before I compete," McKayla admitted to *Teen Vogue*. "I think that everybody does, but when you have more experience, it gets better and better. You learn how to control your nerves."

Of course, the number one question people always asked McKayla concerned her Amanar vault. How did she perform it so spectacularly?

"I've done it for such a long time now that it's like autopilot," she answered. "You just do it."

"I've been working on it for three years," she continued modestly. "Now it's just a vault for me. It's nothing special."

Meanwhile McKayla's coach raved about her smart approach to gymnastics. He had formulated his own theories regarding her success.

"She's a quick learner," he told the *Los Angeles Times*. "She has a natural strength and ability and most importantly, she really wants to do this. She says, 'I want to learn how to do this the correct way.'"

When the clock struck midnight on New Year's Eve, a thrill ran through McKayla's body. With the arrival of 2012 came the London Olympics. After years upon years of anticipation, the excited teen could hardly believe the most important season of her life had finally arrived.

"When you're younger it's just a number to you, and now to be 2012 and know it's finally here is just amazing," she told *International Gymnast Magazine*.

"I started dreaming of going to the Olympics for gymnastics at thirteen," she explained. "I remember watching the girls at the Olympics and knowing I wanted to be there. And having teammates is so important because somebody is there to have your back and cheer you on. I couldn't do it without them."

Before the start of the competitive season, McKayla traveled to Huntsville, Texas, to attend Bela and Marta Karolyi's camp. All the national team members gathered to train their Olympic routines. During down time, she enjoyed socializing with her best friends, Jordyn Wieber and Aly Raisman.

"It's always really fun to see all the girls, and it was a very serious camp," she remarked. "Everybody is training hard and getting ready for the Olympics. All of the girls are pretty much

All Olympia Gymnastics Center
(Joseph Dzidrums)

in 80 percent routine shape, so we're all kind of training our routines that we're going to compete."

McKayla opened the Olympic year strongly by nabbing two gold medals at City of Jesolo Trophy in the team and vault events. A few months later, she flew to Chicago, Illinois, for the Secret U.S. Classic. To no one's surprise, she took the vault title by posting the highest individual score of the competition.

Unfortunately, disaster struck at the 2012 Visa Championships and nearly derailed her Olympic dreams. As McKayla warmed up her floor exercise, during a tumbling pass, she fell back and hit her head. The injured athlete laid on the floor in shock while medics attended to her. Meanwhile, her parents, who witnessed the accident from the stands, rushed to her side.

After a medical team removed McKayla from the competition floor, USA Gymnastics' team doctor examined the teenager and determined that she had suffered a concussion. He ordered her transfer to a local hospital where a CAT Scan could be performed. *NBC* cameras captured heartbreaking video of the tearful two-time world champion being whisked away in an ambulance.

McKayla's injury effectively ended her nationals' participation. At the ER, doctors diagnosed her with a mild concussion and a nasal fracture. Thankfully, USA Gymnastics officials granted her petition for a berth to the Olympic Trials where the five-member London team would be decided.

Another strong candidate for the team? Kyla Ross, whom McKayla befriended at a very young age when she first trained at Gym-Max. The idea that the longtime pals might make the Olympic team together left the world champion breathless.

"That would be like the coolest thing," she told *The Orange County Register*. "When I think about it, it makes me want to cry almost. To have that childhood friend, to have somebody you've worked so hard with, we went through so many things together, to have two girls from the same place like Aliso Viejo to make it to the Olympics would just be awesome."

When McKayla returned home from trials, she had to deal with the frustrating fact that although she had a strong desire to train, her body was not ready. Doctors forbid her from jumping back into training for many days. Eventually, though, she resumed practice a week before leaving for the competition in San Jose.

Fittingly, McKayla began the 2012 Olympic Trials on the vault. 1984 Olympic Champion Tim Daggett sounded breathless with anticipation as the 16-year-old stood at the end of the runway.

"She's going to show us what I believe is unquestionably the greatest vault being performed today by a female gymnast," he raved. "She is the reigning world champion on this vault. She didn't just win in Tokyo last year at worlds, she crushed everybody."

"Nobody flies like her," he added. "Nobody."

Unfortunately, McKayla counted falls on her next two events, the uneven bars and balance beam. She needed a strong floor exercise to get back on track. The resilient competitor delivered with the evening's most graceful routine.

"I'm very pleased with how well she came back from her injury," Marta Karolyi praised. "She is very determined, very aggressive."

"It was really fun out there," McKayla told *NBC* afterwards. "I'm always pretty serious and to myself, so it really looks like I'm nervous, but I actually wasn't too nervous today. I felt pretty calm."

"I messed up on bars and beam so I was definitely a little shocked about that," she continued. "I really tried to hit vault and floor because that's what I'll be contributing to the team at the Olympics, so hopefully that was the good thing for me today. I know on Sunday I have to really come back and do much better."

Forty-eight hours later, McKayla began the second day of trials on the uneven bars. Midway through the routine, she committed a serious form break, but the determined competitor mustered all her strength to remain on the apparatus.

Despite stepping out of bounds on a tumbling pass, McKayla delivered a beautiful floor routine for her third rotation. She then ended the competition on her trademark event, the vault. Yet again she stunned onlookers with her superb vaulting technique.

"That's why she is the greatest vaulter in the world," Tim exclaimed.

After the competition concluded, every gymnast in the building held her breath as Marta Karolyi and other committee members retreated backstage to decide the Olympic team. Five female gymnasts would be sent to the London Games, and McKayla dreamed of hearing her name read as one of the chosen few.

"It's probably the one thing in life that I have wanted forever," she stated nervously. "It's not a puppy that you want for Christmas. It's the Olympics."

A few moments later, the president of USA Gymnastics announced the Olympic team before a packed arena. Among those heading to London? McKayla Maroney!

The emotional gymnast broke down in tears as she celebrated with her Olympic teammates. She would never forget the day for as long as she lived.

"This is the best moment of my whole entire life," she remarked tearfully. "I'm so happy right now."

"We're all best friends," she continued. "We wanted this so bad and we're all in the same boat. We trained so hard. Me and my best friend Kyla…we've been friends since we were seven years old. We did this together. Dreams can come true."

No sooner had McKayla been handed her ticket to London than people began speculating about her medal chances. The remarkable athlete had a legitimate chance to win two gold medals, one as part of the team event and another in the vault finals. When the opportunities arrived, McKayla would be prepared. After all, she had waited for the Olympics for most of her life.

"It's finally here," she smiled. "I'm ready for it."

Competitive Record

National Results

2012 U.S. Olympic Trials
1st-Vault

2012 Visa Championships
W/D

2012 Secret U.S. Classic
1st-Vault

2011 Visa Championships
1st-Vault; 2nd-All-Around

2011 CoverGirl Classic
5th-Floor Exercise

2010 Visa Championships
1st-Vault; 3rd-All-Around; (Jr. Div.)

2010 CoverGirl Classic
2nd-Vault; 7th-All-Around (Jr. Div.)

2009 Visa Championships
3rd-Vault (Jr. Div.)

International Results

2012 City of Jesolo Trophy
1st-Team, Vault; 4th-All-Around

2011 World Championships
1st-Team, Vault

2011 City of Jesolo Trophy
1st-Team, All-Around, Vault

2010 Pan American Championships
1st-Team, Vault, Floor Exercise

"There's nothing better than going out there and seeing USA on your leotard."

"Aly"

On May 25, 1994, in Needham, Massachusetts, Richard and Lynn Raisman took turns cradling their newborn baby. The doting parents gave their daughter the very regal sounding name–Alexandra. Over time, the family called her Aly, for short.

Young and fit, Richard and Lynn were an easygoing couple who lived an active lifestyle. Richard played hockey and baseball, and Lynn competed as a gymnast while in high school. Friends of the couple expected that their children would be athletic, too. Not surprisingly, when Aly was just 18 months old, her mother signed them up for a gymnastics Mommy and Me class.

In the summer of 1996, Lynn sat glued to her television set watching coverage of the Atlanta Olympics. The United States won the most medals of any country during those games with the American women's gymnastics team, dubbed the Magnificent Seven, nabbing perhaps the most memorable victory. An avid gymnastics fan, Lynn recorded the competition, and when it ended, she filed the tape away in her video collection. She had no idea that the recording would one day play a key role in her daughter's life. Around the same time, Richard and Lynn expanded their family with a boy and two more girls.

To no one's surprise, Aly flourished in organized sports having begun classes at Exxcel Gymnastics in Newton. Although the young girl loved learning new skills in practice, she uncovered an even greater passion for competing. The natural performer adored dressing up in a flashy leotard and showing off her acrobatics for an appreciative audience. Although Aly loved the balance beam, vault and uneven bars, the floor exercise thrilled her the most. It felt exhilarating to tumble across the floor unleashing difficult skills that had taken weeks to master.

When Aly turned 10, she started training at Brestyan's American Gymnastics Club under Mihai & Sylvia Brestyan. Mihai's first encounter with the young girl left a strong impression on the Romanian-born coach. The determined gymnast spoke with a confidence well beyond her ten years, and she possessed a big personality that seemed almost too large for her tiny body. The experienced instructor believed both qualities would catapult her far in the sport.

As luck would have it, one of the sport's biggest stars, Alicia Sacramone, also trained at Brestyan's. The much-admired athlete, known for her strong vault and dance skills, would eventually become the most decorated American gymnast in world championship history. The budding gymnast idolized Alicia and felt fortunate to train alongside her hero.

"She's kind of like my older sister," Aly revealed to *NBC*. "I can ask her about anything because I know that she's been through it all. She knows what it takes to get there, so watching her work so hard in the gym everyday is really helpful. I love watching her because she's such a beautiful gymnast, she's so powerful, and has the whole package."

Later that summer, the Raisman family gathered around the television to watch the 2004 Athens Olympics. An enthusiastic Aly reserved most of her cheering for the American girl's gymnastics squad who won the silver medal in the team event.

A few days later, the young gymnast celebrated when Carly Patterson won the all-around crown, and Terin Humphrey, Courtney Kupets and Annia Hatch scored individual medals.

The entire gymnastics competition not only captivated Aly, it inspired her. One evening as the young girl sat watching the competition, she looked at her parents and calmly announced, "I'll be there someday."

Buoyed by Aly's fascination with the Olympics, Lynn dusted off her copy of the 1996 Olympics and played it for her daughter. The starry-eyed gymnast got goose bumps watching the American ladies gymnastics team win gold in a thrilling competition that culminated with Keri Strug's heroic final vault.

"In my room, I would replay it day after day after day," Aly told *NPR*. "And I was literally obsessed with it. I could memorize all the scores and tell you who was going next, and all that stuff. I was so inspired by it."

"She was completely obsessed," Lynn told *The New York Times*. "She watched it again and again and again, and kept telling us how much she wanted to be like those girls. As a parent, you never think your child will actually do everything she says she will, but Aly was different. It was like she wouldn't take no for an answer."

In summer of 2009, Aly qualified for the Visa Championships on the junior level. The country's best gymnasts competed to determine the strongest competitors in each apparatus. Unaffected by the magnitude of the event, the Raisman's oldest daughter captured a balance beam silver medal and an all-around bronze.

Aly Models for GK
(GK)

Richard and Lynn couldn't believe the turn of events. When the down-to-earth parents first enrolled Aly in gymnastics class, they were simply hoping to encourage physical activity. They never dreamed their little girl would become one of the country's top gymnasts!

Aly's national success led to her first international assignment, the Junior Pan American Championships. The fifteen-year-old practically burst with pride when she received her Team USA warm-up suit. She felt honored to travel across the world and represent the United States in such a prestigious competition. In the end, the four-member American team won the team title by nearly 15 points over Canada. Plus, Aly scored three individual medals, including two gold.

"I didn't really know what to expect," she remarked afterwards. "I was really excited because I have been dreaming of representing the USA every since I was a little girl."

The following year, Aly bid goodbye to the junior level. She began her senior career at the Tyson American Cup, not far from home in Worcester. Undaunted by the new level, Aly took all-around silver and vault gold. Performing in front of many family and friends, the appreciative competitor seemed to smile throughout the entire event.

"It's such an honor to even be here," she stated. "I'm so happy. I had so much fun."

After the competition ended, a television reporter asked Aly how she handled the pressure of competing before a home crowd.

"I just tried to block it out and think about the positive... how many people are here cheering me on and how many family and friends I have here," she answered.

Aly's passport received a workout over the next few months. In late March, the teenager helped the U.S. claim team gold at the City of Jesolo Trophy in Italy. A month later, she flew to Melbourne, Australia, for the Pacific Rim Championships and captured three silver medals.

Despite all the traveling that accompanied her burgeoning gymnastics career, Aly remained strongly devoted to her education. She attended classes at Needham High School and cited English as her favorite subject.

"Finding a balance between school and gymnastics can be stressful, [but] they are both important to me," she said.

Aly had the relatively easy commute of flying to Hartford, Connecticut, for the 2010 Visa Championships. The steady competitor reacted to the pressure of competing at her first senior nationals in her usual cool way. She won bronze medals in the all-around, beam and floor exercise.

Aly's dream season only got sweeter when USA Gymnastics named her to the world team. The ecstatic teen flew to Netherlands in early October for her first world championships. Her teammates included: Alicia Sacramone, Rebecca Bross, Mackenzie Caquatto, Bridget Sloan and Mattie Larson.

In the team qualifications, Aly sampled her first taste of world competition. The stakes were higher. The nerves were greater. The crowds were bigger. Aly loved all of it. After round one of competition, the wide-eyed athlete could barely contain her giddiness.

"It was amazing today," she told *USA Gymnastics*. "I had so much fun. I actually wasn't as nervous as I thought I would be. I wasn't even nervous at all. It was a lot of fun."

During team finals, the Americans performed solidly and won the silver medal. Meanwhile, Russia took first place, while China captured the bronze medal.

"Having the silver medal around my neck is really amazing," Aly gushed afterwards. "I had a lot of fun today. I'm very proud of my team. I love them. We all have so much fun together, so I'm really glad to share this special moment with them."

Aly's competition hadn't ended, though. The plucky competitor qualified for the all-around where she placed thirteenth. In addition, she also made floor exercise finals and finished fourth, narrowly missing a medal.

"It's a little bit frustrating," she admitted. "But I'm still very happy with my performance."

Aly may have been a world medalist now, but when she returned home, she remained one of four Raisman children who participated in extracurricular activities. Her brother, Brett, played hockey, and sister Chloe was a horseback rider. Meanwhile, her youngest sibling, Madison, enjoyed a bevy of activities.

"I don't want to be treated any differently," Aly stressed. "I want to be a normal kid like everyone else."

Aly kicked off 2011 by winning a bronze all-around medal at the American Cup. Afterwards she returned to Italy for the City of Jesolo Trophy. Her best friends, Jordyn Wieber and McKayla Maroney also represented the United States. Aly competed remarkably, earning an astonishing five medals, including a team gold.

"Winning the gold medal was an amazing feeling," she told *USA Gymnastics*. "I am really glad that I was able to share the exciting experience with my teammates. I am so lucky to have such great friends like them; we are really close and have so much fun together!"

Around the same time, Aly gained some independence when she acquired her driver's license. Now the sixteen-year-old could drive herself to the gym every day! One afternoon her parents surprised her by presenting her with a Land Rover LR2!

"Aly and her dad were crazy looking for cars," Lynn revealed to *USA Gymnastics*. "She was driving my old car for a while but my husband found this car and knew Aly would love it. We parked the new car in the driveway for her and put a bow on it. Aly was thrilled."

Meanwhile, Aly's gymnastics career continued to soar. At the 2011 CoverGirl Classic, the experienced competitor finished first in the all-around, vault and floor exercise. She felt particularly pleased to land her Amanar, a difficult vault that many gymnasts strive to acquire.

"I'm really excited that I landed my two and half," she smiled. "Even though it wasn't the perfect landing, I still did it!"

A few weeks later, Aly flew to St. Paul, Minnesota, for the 2011 Visa Championships. The steady competitor took home all-around and floor exercise bronze medals.

For the second straight year, Aly earned a spot on the world team. That year's world championships took place in Tokyo, Japan, and the American girls felt determined to bring home gold.

Shortly before the competition, the team suffered a major loss when team captain Alicia Sacramone tore her Achilles tendon. Not only did her injury create a hole in the American lineup, it also left Aly as the surprise team veteran. The mature teen calmly embraced the leadership role and encouraged the girls to snag a victory for Alicia.

"I'm the oldest of all my siblings, so it just kind of came naturally," she told *NBC*. "I didn't really think of it as being the team leader, I just wanted to help the others out."

Over two days' time, the American girls performed effortless looking routines. When the team competition ended, the United States had won gold. Aly and her teammates stood proudly on the podium as organizing officials raised the American flag and played the National Anthem.

"It was a really amazing feeling because I watched the girls in 2003 and 2007 win the gold medal so to be able to be a part of a world championship team is a dream come true," she told *TeamUSA.org*.

"I was just trying to cherish the moment," she added. "I thought about when I was younger when I watched the '96 Olympics and just watching them all stand there with the gold medal and I was doing the same thing."

For the second straight year, Aly qualified for floor exercise finals. Determined to snag the medal she narrowly missed in 2011, she gave a solid performance and finished third!

"It was amazing, I've been waiting so long for that," she told *TeamUSA.org*. "It's definitely a dream come true and hopefully next year there will be a couple more. I mean, I'm always looking to the next thing, it's never good enough because I always want to do more and it always makes me more determined to do better next time."

Now the proud owner of a full set of world championship medals, Aly returned home to great fanfare. Of course, those closest to her weren't surprised by her enormous success.

"Gymnastics has really taken a priority in her life for a really long time, and that comes from her," Lynn said. "Because if it didn't, I think she would have quit a long time ago."

"I don't think she necessarily gets enough credit for how well she competes," claimed Alicia Sacramone. "At the last two world championships, I don't think she's made any mistakes. She's the backbone. If you want her to go and do something, do a solid routine, she's going to do it."

Now a world champion gymnast, Aly saw her fan base skyrocket. She gained thousands of *Twitter* and *Facebook* followers. Her diverse fan base came from all over the world including: Mexico, Germany and Israel.

Aly knew how it felt to admire a public figure. For instance, she liked Taylor Swift and listened to her music all the time. She even cited the haunting "Enchanted" as her favorite song.

Around the same time, Aly made a major decision regarding her gymnastics career. She opted to turn professional which would allow her to receive prize money and monetary compensation for endorsements. Almost instantly, she signed a deal with GK Elite to model their leotards in various print publications. She also posed for a Got Milk? ad and signed on for the much-anticipated Kellogg's Tour of Gymnastics Champions.

When Aly rang in 2012 a few months later, the high school senior felt restless with anticipation. The Olympic season had finally arrived. She had dreamed of the year for so long.

"I'm excited," she told *NPR*. "I'm anxious. And I'm just kind of ready for it to happen. I feel like I've been waiting my whole life for it. So I just kind of want it to come now."

Although the Americans were the reigning world champions, Aly wasn't taking a victory for granted. She expected a tough battle in London.

"I don't want to get too cocky," she cautioned. "The Russians, Romanians and Chinese have amazing gymnasts. You never know what they're going to have in a year, so we all just have to go home and work hard."

When the 2012 competition season began, Aly continued solidifying her status as a model of composure and consistency. She placed second at the American Cup and scooped up three medals at the City of Jesolo Trophy.

A few weeks later, Aly also won the all-around and balance beam honors at the Secret U.S. Classic. The victory came as a belated birthday present for the steady competitor. She turned 18 the previous day.

"I celebrated by having a good competition today," she smiled. "That was kind of what I was going for the whole day. Yesterday I used my birthday as motivation because I didn't want to mess up. I didn't want it to ruin my birthday, so every time I went up, I thought about doing it as perfect as possible so I could be happy."

Aly felt thrilled to score over 60 points in the all-around. However, the hardworking gymnast was not about to rest on her laurels.

"I can't wait to go back to the gym and keep working harder than ever before," she stated.

The competition also marked the comeback of one of Aly's heroes. 2008 Olympic All-Around Champion Nastia Liukin returned to competition in the first step toward her attempt to make the 2012 London Olympics.

"Having her back out on the floor was really weird because I never competed with her before," Aly gushed. "I always used to watch her and look up to her. To have her there, it's really fun. She did so great out there tonight. I'm so happy for her. She deserved it. She worked so hard."

In the meantime, gymnastics insiders continued to praise Aly's remarkable steadiness. Time after time, the determined athlete nailed her routines.

"She is just so solid," raved National Team Coordinator Marta Karolyi. "She goes out there and doesn't act like she's bothered by anything. She knows she's trained, she knows she's ready and she doesn't put any extra pressure on herself."

"I really love to have this kind of gymnast," she added. "She gives her heart."

Aly clearly deserved her reputation as one of the world's best competitors. When people often asked her for tips on battling competition nerves, she offered straightforward advice.

"I try not to over think it," she said simply. "When you over think it, you mess it up more."

When Aly landed in St. Louis, Missouri, for the 2012 Visa Championships, she carried a very specific wish. She wanted to win a national title.

On her last event of the competition, as Aly attempted a split jump, she glanced out into the audience and met her mother's eyes. It was a moment worthy of goose bumps. The woman who introduced the world champion to gymnastics sat watching her compete in one of the biggest competitions of her life.

"I normally don't like to see her when I compete," Aly remarked. "I was nervous that it was going to mess me up but it was fine. It was weird. For one second I looked up and she was the one person I saw."

At the event's conclusion, Aly got her wish by earning, not one, but two gold medals on balance beam and floor exercise. She also placed third in the all-around.

"I'm so excited with how I did today," she told *NBC*. "I know that I still have more room for improvement but I feel good with where I am going into Olympic trials."

"I'm just really happy that I finally won a national title," she added. "It really means the world to me."

Meanwhile Aly's personal life experienced momentous events. For starters, she attended prom with a good friend. The clothes-obsessed teen, who planned to someday study fashion design in college, took great care when selecting a gown for the occasion. She finally chose a brown dress with a v-neck and cap sleeves with jewels.

"It's very simple, and elegant and sophisticated," she told *NPR*. "I'm really excited to wear it."

A few months later, Aly also graduated from high school. When the hardworking gymnast and student walked onto the stage to receive her diploma, her class showered her with a standing ovation.

"I'm officially not in high school anymore which is really crazy," the new graduate said almost in disbelief as she smiled slightly.

Aly didn't have much time to celebrate, though. She hit the gym every day in preparation for the 2012 Olympic Trials where the London team would be named. One of her competitors at trials would be best friend Jordyn Wieber.

"Competing against Jordyn is always a great experience," she told *WILX.com*. "I think that we both push each other to the next level. Even though we're competing against each other, we both want each other to do really well. I have so much respect for her. She works so hard and is such an amazing competitor."

"She's my best friend even though she lives in Michigan and I live in Boston," she continued. "When we're not doing gymnastics, we still keep in touch even though we live so far away. We text basically every day and it's really great because we're both striving for the same goal."

As Aly prepared for the most important competition of her life, she knew that her mental approach mattered almost as much as her physical approach.

"I'm just going to go in there very confident and make sure that my routines are very consistent and just do the same thing I've been doing my whole life," she remarked.

"Obviously I've never been to an Olympic trials before so I'm really excited about that," she said.

Wearing a sparkly purple leotard on the competition's day one, Aly displayed her trademark consistency. The Olympic hopeful completed a solid Amanar vault in round one. She followed that with relatively clean uneven bars and balance beam performances.

"Marta Karolyi loves her," *NBC* sportscaster Elfi Schlegel remarked. "She loves her mental toughness."

At the competition's midpoint, Aly sat in third place in the all-around. She was halfway toward an Olympic berth.

"Being here at the Olympic Trials is such a dream come true and such an honor," she said afterwards. "I'm so happy to be here. I had so much fun competing out there today. I can't wait for Sunday because I still have room to improve."

On the afternoon of day two of trials, Aly went out to lunch with several of her gymnast friends, including Jordyn Wieber and Nastia Liukin. During a break in the conversation, the avid tweeter checked her *Twitter* account and then did a double take. Boston Bruin Tyler Seguin had wished her good luck in the competition. The NHL hockey fan was so excited that Jordyn and Nastia began playfully teasing her over her enthusiasm!

NBC broadcast live coverage of the nail-biting night two of competition. Dressed in a red leotard with blue sleeves, Aly performed consistently on her first event, the uneven bars. She battled the balance beam next and produced another solid performance. For her third event, she delivered a crowd-pleasing floor routine. Her only blemish of the evening came with a slight stumble on the vault. Still it didn't seem serious enough to jeopardize her chances of making the London team.

"If she's not on the Olympic team, I have no idea what they're thinking," remarked 1984 Olympic Champion Tim Daggett.

Moments later Aly and the other girls sat backstage in a holding room awaiting word on which lucky gymnasts would travel to London. As the girls fidgeted nervously, Alicia Sacramone tried to lighten the mood by playing music for the tense room. Finally Marta Karolyi entered the room carrying a sheet of paper.

"The 2012 Olympic Team is: Gabby Douglas, McKayla Maroney, Aly Raisman, Kyla Ross and Jordyn Wieber."

The usually composed Aly broke down in tears upon hearing her name. She placed her hand over her heart and began hyperventilating.

"I haven't cried like that in a very, very long time, like ever since I was a little girl," she later remarked. "It was really emotional."

Before the new Olympians had a chance to absorb the news, USA Gymnastics officials ordered them back into the arena to be introduced to the waiting audience. As the five girls marched onto the stage while their names were called, the crowd roared for the new Olympians.

Afterwards the emotional teenager still wiped away tears as she spoke with reporters.

"I'm so excited to be on the Olympic team," she cried. "July 1 is the greatest day of my life."

At least until the day she competes in the Olympics.

Competitive Record

National Results

2012 U.S. Olympic Trials
3rd-All-Around; 1st-Balance Beam, Floor Exercise

2012 Visa Championships
1st-Balance Beam, Floor Exercise; 3rd-All-Around

2012 Secret U.S. Classic
1st-All-Around, Balance Beam, Floor Exercise; 2nd-Vault

2011 Visa Championships
3rd-All-Around, Floor Exercise

2011 CoverGirl Classic
1st-All-Around, Vault, Floor Exercise; 3rd-Balance Beam

2010 Visa Championships
3rd-All-Around, Balance Beam, Floor Exercise

2010 CoverGirl Classic
5th-All-Around

2009 Visa Championships
2nd-Balance Beam; 3rd-All-Around (Jr. Div.)

2009 CoverGirl Classic
3rd-Floor Exercise (Jr. Div.)

2009 American Classic
1st-Vault; 10th-All-Around (Jr. Div.)

International Results

2012 City of Jesolo Trophy
1st-Team; 2nd-All-Around, Floor Exercise; 3rd-Uneven Bars

2012 AT&T American Cup
2nd-All-Around

2011 World Championships
1st-Team; 3rd-Floor Exercise; 4th-All-Around

2011 City of Jesolo Trophy
1st-Team, Balance Beam, Floor Exercise; 3rd-All-Around, Vault

2011 AT&T American Cup
3rd-All-Around

2010 World Championships
2nd-Team

2010 Pacific Rim Championships
1st-Team; 2nd-All-Around, Balance Beam, Floor Exercise

2010 City of Jesolo Trophy
1st-Team, All-Around

2010 Tyson American Cup
2nd-All-Around

2009 Junior Pan American Championships
1st-Team, Vault, Floor Exercise; 3rd-All-Around

Eat the competition for breakfast. With milk.

Our athletes know that getting the right nutrients first thing in the morning is golden.

:BreakfastProject.com

Nourish every day.

"It's always a little girl's dream to say they want to compete in the Olympics."

"MIGHTY MOUSE"

Rugged Jason Ross played baseball and football at University of Hawaii. One day while on campus, he noticed a pretty student named Kiana and introduced himself to her. After many months of dating, the couple fell in love and married shortly afterwards.

After his college days ended, Jason found himself drafted by the Atlanta Braves. For six years he played for the baseball team's minor league affiliate. In fact, the talented outfielder advanced all the way up to Triple-A baseball.

On October 24, 1996, in a Honolulu hospital, Kiana gave birth to a baby daughter. The proud parents named her Kyla, which means "beautiful and graceful." The happy pair would later add two more children to their family, Mckenna and Kayne.

Baby Kyla learned to climb before she could walk. Armed with relentless energy, the tiny girl rarely stopped moving and learned to scale the family sofa at an amazingly young age.

On some days, Kiana would give her furniture a break and take her daughter to the park for additional exercise. Kyla, still just a baby, would climb to the highest point of the jungle gym, alarming the other mothers on the playground.

"There's a baby stuck on the top of the jungle gym!" a concerned mom would shriek in terror.

"That's my baby," Kiana would answer calmly. "She's fine. She's an experienced climber. She does this all the time."

The other parents would shake their heads in awe and disbelief. They had never seen a baby who could move like such a professional at such a young age.

While living in Greenville, South Carolina, at the time, Jason and Kiana enrolled their three-year-old in a recreational gymnastics class. The duo hoped to channel the young girl's hyperactivity into a positive outlet.

Of course, Kyla's parents never dreamed their actions would lead to their daughter becoming a force in gymnastics. Gymnasts were tiny and compact. At the lanky height of 6'5", Jason fully expected his child would inherit his tall genes.

"Maybe she'll become a volleyball player someday," he always thought.

Right off the bat, Kyla's coach noticed the young girl possessed remarkable strength, an enormous attribute in gymnastics. Meanwhile, the tiny gymnast loved her regular visits to the gym. With four different apparatuses to capture her attention, she never grew bored!

Shortly before Kyla turned five years old, her father retired from baseball. The Ross family then moved to Southern California where they had family. When they settled in Orange County, Jason found work as a sales rep, while Kiana worked various odd jobs.

As luck would have it, the Ross family lived near a wonderful gymnastics club named Gym-Max. Owned by the husband and wife team of Howie Liang and Jenny Zhang, the training center produced many champions over the years. In fact, many years earlier, Liang had coached Chow, Shawn Johnson and Gabby's Douglas' famed coach!

When Liang took one look at Kyla, he noticed she had an unusual body. For starters, the petite girl appeared very boxy which would give her gymnastics much power. On the other hand, she also possessed long, balletic lines, too.

"I think that's why Howie kind of took to her," Kiana told the *Los Angeles Times*.

Shortly after arriving at the Orange County facility, Kyla met another gymnast named McKayla Maroney. The two girls became fast friends and carved a friendship that would last throughout their elite years, even after McKayla would switch gyms many years later.

"They compliment each other as friends," Kiana told *The Orange County Register*. "They bring out the best in each other."

"We're still best friends," McKayla once said. "We're so close. We pretty much know everything about each other. That's what happens when you grow up together, when you're in the gym with somebody all day."

Over the next few years, Kyla advanced through levels one through ten at a swift pace, culminating with the Level 10 National Championships in Orlando, Florida. The gifted gymnast dominated the competition by winning the all-around, uneven bars and balance beam titles. She also snagged the vault silver medal.

Every time Kyla returned from a competition with new hardware, it only motivated her to work harder in the gym.

Kyla charms the crowd
(AP)

If the focused athlete had to pick a favorite event to train, she liked balance beam the best. In her eyes, the tricky apparatus showcased what she loved most about gymnastics.

"I have always loved beam because I feel it is extremely challenging every time you get on it," she told *GKElite.com*. "I also find that it showcases the most grace and perfection with every move you make."

In the summer of 2009, Kyla qualified for the Visa Championships in Dallas, Texas. At the tender age of 12, the resilient junior competitor won the all-around gold medal over many gymnasts much older than her.

"I was definitely nervous," she remarked after the competition. "It was my first time so everything was like really new. I didn't know what to expect, so I just went out there and gave it my best."

In the fall of that year, Kyla received her first international assignment. She flew to Aracaju, Brazil, to compete at the Junior Pan American Championships. Not intimidated by the big stage, the young gymnast won all-around, balance beam and uneven bars gold medals. She also helped the U.S. to a team victory.

One year later, Kyla successfully defended her title at the 2010 Visa Championships in Hartford, Connecticut. In fact, she won the championship by more than two points over silver medalist Katelyn Ohashi. She also added a bronze balance beam medal to her blossoming resume.

Around this time, a national coach became so impressed by Kyla's strength and power that he nicknamed her Mighty Mouse. The cute name stuck and would follow the gymnast throughout her career.

Although Kyla dedicated herself 100% toward her gymnastics career, she cherished her school experience as well. While many gymnasts opt to either do home schooling or take online classes, the dedicated teen insisted on attending classes at Aliso Niguel High School. Of course, her choice meant that she often rose at 5:30 every morning to finish that day's homework. The practical teen listed biology and math as her favorite subjects. She also considered herself an avid reader and especially loved the *Hunger Games* series.

In 2011 Kyla flew to Italy to compete in the City of Jesolo Trophy which delighted her. The focused teen considered it a great honor to represent her country in international competition. Thanks to Kyla's integral contributions, the United States handily won the team title. In addition, the Southern

California resident also scooped up all-around and balance beam gold medals.

"It was exciting being able to travel to Italy," she told *USA Gymnastics*. "The plane ride was long but I had fun being with such a large group of girls the whole trip."

"The best part of the trip was getting to shop and ride the gondola in Venice, and of course winning the team gold," she added.

Kyla also enjoyed the camaraderie that accompanied a team competition. She enjoyed getting to know the other senior competitors and found herself making lasting friendships with her American teammates.

"I just think getting to know each other well and having fun together helps in the gym because we cheer each other on and we just want to be all part of Team USA," she remarked.

Now that Kyla had carved a strong reputation on the international level, the Olympics suddenly seemed like a plausible reality for the youngster. She desperately dreamed of competing in the 2012 London Games. To remind herself of her goal, the determined athlete printed a copy of the Olympics gymnastics schedule and kept it by her bed.

"If I'm feeling good one day, or I might not have the best day, I try to look at it for some motivation," she told *The Orange County Register*.

After competing as a junior for three straight seasons, Kyla moved up to the senior level in 2012. She felt happy to leave the junior ranks behind.

"I am really excited to finally compete as a senior now and to compete in front of a bigger audience and show myself and my gymnastics," she revealed to *NBC*. "I've been a junior for a long time."

Although Kyla was a rookie on the senior level, she viewed the 2012 Olympic season with high hopes. Right away the hard-working teen set her sights on competing in the London Games.

"I should be on the team," she told the *Los Angeles Times*. "I hit my routines. They have good start values. I'm consistent. That's what I bring. So they should bring me."

Meanwhile, Kyla discovered that she had a big fan in a gymnastics legend. Shannon Miller, the most decorated gymnast in U.S. history, picked her as the one to watch during the Olympic season.

"She is absolutely incredible," Shannon raved.

The admiration went both ways. When asked whose career she would like to emulate, Kyla answered Shannon Miller because of her success at the Olympics. In fact, Shannon was her favorite gymnast ever.

"In addition to her numerous gymnastics achievements, she is a strong woman who has faced personal hardships, but continued to stay involved in the gymnastics world," she told *NBC*.

St. Louis, Missouri, hosted the 2012 Visa Championships. Before the competition began, the *NBC* on-air crew interviewed National Team Coordinator Marta Karolyi, the woman responsible for choosing the Olympic team. Before the sportscasters finished asking the influential woman about her thoughts on various gymnasts, she interrupted them with her own question.

"Well, what about Kyla Ross?" she asked before proceeding to gush over the youngster's gymnastics.

There are many adjustments a gymnast makes when transitioning to the senior level. For starters, the media makes their presence felt everywhere. On day one of her first senior nationals, television cameras followed Kyla's every move.

Of course, the mental approach plays a greater role in senior events, too. To put it simply, the stakes are higher at the top level.

"To compete in such a big meet is hard to keep your emotions straight," Kyla acknowledged before the competition.

Perhaps distracted by the additional pressure, the usually focused competitor began strongly on her first apparatuses but then made an uncharacteristic mistake on her floor exercise. She stepped out of bounds on her first tumbling pass during her routine to *The Phantom of the Opera* score.

"There are a lot of things I could have done better," she remarked after day one of competition. "I think I had a pretty clean meet. Hopefully I'll come back Sunday and come back even stronger."

"And I'm going to stay on the floor this time," she vowed.

On the competition's second day, which happened to also fall on her father's birthday, Kyla donned a patriotic red, white and blue leotard courtesy of GK Elite. She began her journey on the uneven bars.

"What makes her so special are the beautiful lines that she will show off on this event," raved *NBC* commentator Elfi Schlegel at the start of Kyla's uneven bars routine.

The steady gymnast delivered a strong, confident routine with exquisite form and impressive release skills. When she stuck her landing, her coach pumped his fist triumphantly.

"That was really a great start for day two for Kyla Ross," 1984 Olympic Champion Tim Daggett proclaimed. "Exactly what Marta Karolyi expects…demands."

Kyla moved to the balance beam next. Though she committed a few bobbles and balance checks, the teenager gave an otherwise solid performance.

"It was a very strong routine overall," Tim remarked. "Overall, that would do very well at an international event."

For her third event, Kyla faced the floor exercise. This time the determined athlete remained in bounds on all her tumbling passes. When she ended her routine, the appreciative audience showered her with loud applause.

"Good job," Marta exclaimed with approval.

"Powerful music," Elfi commented. "That piece really carries Kyla throughout this routine. I love it."

"She is a strong competitor on all four events," Tim praised. "She just showed again that she can deal with that pressure."

For her final apparatus, Kyla displayed a solid vault. In the end, she finished a respectable fourth in the all-around competition. She also scored her first senior national medal when she took silver on the uneven bars event.

Kyla's top four placement qualified her for the Olympic Trials in San Jose, California. Immediately following nationals, she returned home and began training for the competition that would decide the London team.

Sometimes after a tiring training session, Kyla would unwind in front of the television and watch her favorite show *So You Think You Can Dance.* Other times she enjoyed a DVD starring her favorite actress Sandra Bullock. She particularly liked the romantic comedy *The Proposal.*

On some occasions, the fifteen-year-old needed to blow off steam or release tension. In those instances, she turned to her iPod playlist for comfort. Her favorite artists included: One Direction, Rihanna, Beyonce, P. Diddy, and Justin Bieber.

Wearing a pretty pink leotard, Kyla marched confidently into the HP Pavilion for day one of Olympic Trials. Although she was a first year senior, many considered her a strong bet to make the London team.

"If the USA has a weakness, it's on the uneven bars," remarked Tim. "Being that Kyla Ross is one of the top workers in the U.S. on the uneven bars. . .with her sturdy all-around performance…that is a wonderful recipe to becoming an Olympian."

On a warm summer night in Northern California, Kyla began her Olympic quest on the uneven bars. The reigning U.S. silver medalist on the apparatus, she delivered one of the competition's most difficult routines and made it look easy.

"She has the international look that the judges around the world crave," Tim pointed out. "Long, lean, clean lines."

Kyla competed next on the balance beam where she stuck her landing perfectly. Then she also hit her third event, the floor exercise.

"She is having herself a very good night," remarked *NBC* commentator Al Trautwig.

Finally, Kyla ended the night on the vault. Unfortunately, while performing the difficult Amanar, she struggled on her landing and fell to the mat. Her mistake dropped her from third to fifth overall.

"I was pretty happy except for vault," Kyla told *The Orange County Register*. "I thought I came out with a pretty good competition. I was consistent on other events and I just need to clean up a few bobbles on beam and hopefully I can come back and do a better vault on Sunday."

On night two of trials, donning a stunning red leotard, Kyla unleashed a solid vault for her first apparatus. She then traveled to the uneven bars and delivered a breathtaking routine packed with difficulty.

"That was fantastic," Tim exclaimed. "That was big time pressure for Kyla Ross and she delivered."

When the London hopeful walked off the floor, her coach patted her back with great enthusiasm. Meanwhile she also impressed a fellow competitor. 2008 Olympic All-Around Champion Nastia Liukin offered her congratulations and a big hug.

For her third event, Kyla would face the balance beam. Despite performing on a four-inch wide apparatus, the California native looked fearless, aggressive and graceful during her routine. She broke into a huge grin upon nailing her dismount.

"This is the type of gymnastics that has traditionally scored very well on the international stage," Elfi remarked.

Kyla competed the floor exercise on her final rotation. Looking poised beyond her years, she hit every tumbling pass and struck her final pose with great confidence.

"It's a great moment for Kyla," Elfi said.

"She did all she could today," Tim agreed.

With eight routines behind her, Kyla's Olympic future now rested in the hands of a committee who would decide the team. Moments later, she and her teammates sat backstage and held their breath anxiously. Finally Marta entered the room and read the names of the athletes chosen for the Olympic team: Gabby Douglas, McKayla Maroney, Aly Raisman, Kyla Ross and Jordyn Wieber.

Kyla Ross! The tiny dynamo from Southern California had accomplished her lifelong dream! She was going to London!

A few moments later, the enormity of the situation still hadn't hit Kyla. The overwhelmed teenager had difficulty putting her emotions into words.

"It's something that's really indescribable," she said. "We've all been working so hard for this moment. Hearing our names called…none of us could even believe it. We were just so proud of all of us and how hard all of the girls competed out here."

"I'm just so glad and happy," she remarked. "I've worked so hard for this moment and I'm ready for London."

Kyla's Training Center
(Joseph Dzidrums)

Competitive Record

National Results

2012 U.S. Olympic Trials
1st-Uneven Bars; 3rd-Balance Beam

2012 Visa Championships
2nd-Uneven Bars; 4th-All-Around

2012 Secret U.S. Classic
2nd-All-Around, Uneven Bars

2011 Visa Championships
2nd-All-Around, Uneven Bars, Balance Beam; 3rd-Vault (Jr. Div.)

2011 CoverGirl Classic
1st-All-Around, Uneven Bars; 2nd-Vault; 3rd-Floor Exercise (Jr. Div.)

2010 Visa Championships
1st-All-Around, Balance Beam; 3rd-Vault, Floor Exercise (Jr. Div.)

2010 CoverGirl Classic
1st-Balance Beam (Jr. Div.)

2009 Visa Championships
1st-All-Around, Vault, Balance Beam; 3rd-Floor Exercise (Jr. Div.)

2009 CoverGirl Classic
1st-All-Around, Vault (Jr. Div.)

2009 American Classic
1st-Balance Beam; 2nd-All-Around; 3rd-Vault, Floor Exercise (Jr. Div.)

2008 Level 10 National Championships
1st-All-Around, Balance Beam, Floor Exercise; 2nd-Vault (Jr. A)

International Results

2012 City of Jesolo Trophy
1st-Team, All-Around, Uneven Bars, Balance Beam; 3rd-Vault

2012 Kellogg's Pacific Rim Championships
1st-Team, Balance Beam; 2nd-All-Around, Uneven Bars; 3rd-Floor Exercise

2011 City of Jesolo Trophy
1st-Team, All-Around, Balance Beam; 2nd-Vault, Uneven Bars (Jr. Div.)

2010 Pan American Championships
1st-Team, All-Around; 2nd-Floor Exercise

2010 Pacific Rim Championships
1st-Team, Vault; 2nd-All-Around, Uneven Bars, Floor Exercise (Jr. Div.)

2010 City of Jesolo Trophy
2nd-All-Around (Jr. Div.)

2009 Junior Pan American Championships
1st-Team, All-Around, Uneven Bars, Balance Beam; 2nd-Floor Exercise

In the event that Jordyn, Gabby, McKayla, Aly or Kyla are unable to compete in London, USA Gymnastics named three replacement athletes to the team. Here's the lowdown on these talented young women.

Sarah Finnegan

Born on November 14, 1996, tiny Sarah Finnegan hails from St. Louis, Missouri. The daughter of Don and Linabelle Finnegan, she initially began taking gymnastics just for fun and discovered she had a great talent for it. Sarah isn't the only gymnast in her family. Her sisters, Hannah, Jennah, and Aleah, are also gymnasts!

An all-around gymnast, Sarah's favorite events are balance beam and floor exercise. She is best known for her 'triple Terin turn', which she performs on both apparatuses. The fifteen-year-old named the skill after Terin Humphrey, the two-time Olympic silver medalist, who was the first to perform it. She has something else in common with the former competitor. Like Sarah, Terin was also coached by Al Fong and Armine Barutyan-Fong at GAGE [Great American Gymnastics Express] in Kansas City.

"Watching them is going to be so exciting, and cheering the team on," Sarah said when asked about being named an Olympic alternate. "If I do get to compete, hopefully we'll bring some medals home."

Anna Li

Anna Li was born in Las Vegas, Nevada, on September 4, 1988, to Yuejiu Li and Jiani Wu. Both parents, who also coach their daughter, competed for China at the 1984 Summer Olympics. Anna began gymnastics at age four when she visited her parents at the gym where they coached and begged for a leotard. They told her she couldn't wear one unless she competed so the young girl began taking lessons.

A stellar uneven bars worker, Anna returned to elite gymnastics in 2010 after a successful NCAA career. She competed on the collegiate level for UCLA where she led the team to a championship in 2010. After graduating with a history degree, she resumed elite gymnastics and was selected as an alternate on the 2011 world championship team.

"I was in shock," she told the *Chicago Tribune* about hearing her name called as an Olympic alternate. "My name was announced and I didn't expect to hear it! I was just so happy. I did my routines to the best of my own capabilities. So, regardless of the outcome, I knew I had no regrets!"

Elizabeth Price

Born on May 25, 1996, Elizabeth Price's parents, David and Diane, first placed her in a gymnastics class with the hope that it would tire the three-year-old out! The talented teen hails from an athletic family. Her father was a soccer player, while her mom played volleyball. Meanwhile, her brothers, Ethan and Elijan, play several sports.

An all-around gymnast, Elizabeth trains at Parkette's National Training Center with Donna and Bill Strauss.

Although the exciting gymnast boasts explosive vaulting ability, she considers uneven bars and floor exercise her favorite events. Prior to her fourth-place all-around finish at trials, Elizabeth placed fifth in the all-around at the 2012 Visa Championships. The sixteen-year-old is nicknamed: Ebee.

"I'm really excited to go to London," she told *The Morning Call.* "I think I'm most excited about representing my gym at the Olympics."

Sarah Finnegan
(Getty)

Christine Dzidrums holds a bachelor's degree in Theater Arts from California State University, Fullerton. She previously wrote the biographies: *Joannie Rochette: Canadian Ice Princess, Yuna Kim: Ice Queen, Shawn Johnson: Gymnastics' Golden Girl* and *Nastia Liukin: Ballerina of Gymnastics.* Her first novel, *Cutters Don't Cry,* won a 2010 Moonbeam Children's Book Award in the Young Adult Fiction category. She also wrote the tween book, *Fair Youth,* and the beginning reader books, *Timmy and the Baseball Birthday Party* and *Timmy Adopts a Girl Dog.* Christine also authored the picture book, *Princess Dessabelle Makes a Friend.* She recently competed her second novel, *Kaylee: The 'What If?' Game.*

Shawn Johnson, the young woman from Des Moines, Iowa, captivated the world at the 2008 Beijing Olympics when she snagged a gold medal on the balance beam.

Shawn Johnson: Gymnastics' Golden Girl, the first volume in the **GymnStars** series, chronicles the life and career of one of sport's most beloved athletes.

Widely considered America's greatest gymnast ever, **Nastia Liukin** has inspired an entire generation with her brilliant technique, remarkable sportsmanship and unparalleled artistry.

A children's biography, *Nastia Liukin: Ballerina of Gymnastics* traces the Olympic all-around champion's ascent from gifted child prodigy to queen of her sport.

Also From

2010 Moonbeam Children's Book Award Winner! In a series of raw journal entries written to her absentee father, a teenager chronicles her penchant for self-harm, a serious struggle with depression and an inability to vocally express her feelings.

"I play the 'What If?'" game all the time. It's a cruel, wicked game."

Meet free spirit Kaylee Matthews, the most popular girl in school. But when the teenager suffers a devastating loss, her sunny personality turns dark as she struggles with debilitating panic attacks and unresolved anger. Can Kaylee repair her broken spirit, or will she forever remain a changed person?

Meet **Princess Dessabelle**, a spoiled, lonely princess with a quick temper. When she orders a kind classmate to be her friend, she learns the true meaning of friendship.

Build Your Timmy™
Collection Today!

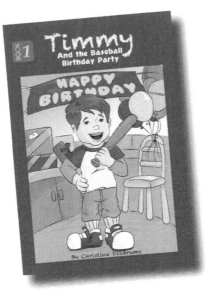

Meet 4½ year old Timmy Martin! He's the biggest baseball fan in the world.

Imagine Timmy's excitement when he gets invited to his cousin's birthday party. Only it's not just any old birthday party... It's a baseball birthday party!

Timmy and the Baseball Birthday Party is the first book in a series of stories featuring the world's most curious little boy!

Timmy Martin has always wanted a dog. Imagine his excitement when his mom and dad agree to let him adopt a pet from the animal shelter. Will Timmy find the perfect dog? And will his new pet know how to play baseball?

Timmy Adopts A Girl Dog is the second story in the series about the world's most curious 4½ year old.

Twelve-year-old Emylee Markette has felt invisible her entire life. Then one fateful afternoon, three beautiful sisters arrive in her sleepy New England town and instantly become the most popular girls at Forest Springs Middle School. To everyone's surprise, the Fay sisters befriend Emylee and welcome her into their close-knit circle. Before long, the shy loner finds herself running with the cool crowd, joining the track team and even becoming friends with her lifelong crush.

Through it all, though, Emylee's weighed down by nagging suspicions. Why were the Fay sisters so anxious to befriend her? How do they know some of her inner thoughts? What do they truly want from her?

When Emylee eventually discovers that her new friends are secretly fairies, she finds her life turned upside down yet again and must make some life-changing decisions.

Fair Youth: Emylee of Forest Springs marks the first volume in an exciting new book series.

Made in the USA
Lexington, KY
12 September 2012